Spiritual Journey ~ Story of An Adopted Child

Christine Guardiano

For information write:

Christine Guardiano Publishing
42 Old East Neck Rd.
Melville, NY 11747

Or call: 631-673-6092
Email: growinlite@hotmail.com

Publishing House: www.InstantPublisher.com

Library of Congress Catalog Card Number: 2006931080
ISBN 1-59872-519-X
10 9 8 7 6 5 4 3 2 1

Dedication

This book is dedicated to Roger and Doris Higgins.

Acknowledgments

Thank you to my family and friends
for all of their love and support ~
Especially Jayne Rhodes

A Special Thank You
To
Steven Cohn
whom without his constant energy and talent,
this book would never have come to fruition

Foreword
by the author's daughter

A few years ago, my mother told me she was planning on writing a book, and asked me how I felt about it because I would be a large part of the story. When she first told me the idea, I honestly thought she would never make the time or have the energy to do it; and even if she did, what could possibly inspire her to achieve such a feat? Now, I know exactly what it was that kept her inspired, because it's exactly what she has taught me my entire life.... that people, moments, and even hardships can make us want to achieve things, but deep down what inspires us the most is our own life. She taught me that life is enough to make us want to do anything, that there is no more of a reason to want to fulfill our dreams. And as you will read, Life has not only made my mom accomplish her dream, but I am sure at the same time, it has given her a huge incentive to keep going, to keep believing, to keep being inspired. And I am so glad that she has found an inspiration, much as I have found with her as an example. And with that, there is a purpose for everything in life.

~ Holly,
March 6, 2006

About Christine...

by the author's spiritual mentor and friend

It is with a great deal of pleasure that I share with you my knowledge of Christine. I have known Chris for about ten years and have observed her spiritual growth and been a recipient of her many talents.

Her bright eyes, pleasant appearance, and personality are like Spring: displaying a blossoming smile, dancing eyes, and creative skills. Expressions of her strong beliefs and generosity will enhance each person's experience with Chris. Her ability as a poetress and creator of labyrinths is like Summer: warming, relaxing, and inviting (to submerge oneself in deep inner thought).

Christine's talents seem almost unlimited. Her creative skills are like Christmas morning opening up hidden treasures, bringing sheer delight to the receiver. Her poetry, dancing, and beading, to name a few, have brought much happiness.

So, to me, Chris is an all-season gal, and I am proud and grateful to call her a special friend and spiritual sister. I wish her well with her book and I am sure you will enjoy walking with her through her life, which she is sharing.

-- Ellie Fristensky

Preface
by the author

From what I understand, many people get an itch
to write a book sometime in their fifties.
An itch would not describe the case with me.
It's not that I had never thought
about the possibility of writing a book,
it was that it just seemed like something
I couldn't do or would never do.
This book was written
thanks to the guidance of the universal forces,
those from beyond and those on this earth.
Every word was Divinely guided
and each sentence was a joy.
Although it took a lot of dedication and time,
I never felt stressed, stuck, or confused during the process.
It was as if Spirit was guiding each step as I wrote
and brought the book into completion.
If I needed help or another opinion from someone,
that person would be there to assist me.
Once the Force gave me the insight
as to what the book should be about,
I knew that it was important for me to write it.
My intention was to reach those on this earth
working with abandonment issues,
and not just children who are adopted.
I wanted to touch those
who feel isolated, depressed, or unworthy of living.
I had those feelings too in my life,
and at the time,
prayed that someone, or something somewhere
would help me.
So this is my personal hope and intent
in writing this book:
to reach those who are disheartened,
and to let them know that they are not alone.
If I touch one person with my story,
my life will be touched too.

Introduction

Kathy Jane Segur, Christine Diane Higgins, Christine Guardiano... Yes, to all of these names I will answer. Yet what answers did they hold for me in my life? Did I have loving parents to bring me up? Yes, but they were not able to help me find my own self-worth. That was my job as an adopted child: to find out where I belonged on this planet.

As a young child, I felt worthless, good-for-nothing, as they might say. No confidence, no strength, no power within myself to make my life seem worthwhile. How could I feel this way, you might ask, when my adopted parents loved me so much and gave me everything they could?

It was my purpose here on earth to work though this rejection and feeling of abandonment. This I learned as I grew spiritually with the one hand that held onto mine and never let go: God's hand. It was always with me, even when I felt he was so far away. He helped me find the strength I needed to make something of my life and myself. He saw me through finding my mother dead, yet very much alive in the face of my reincarnated daughter. He gave me great understanding beyond my wildest dreams. Read my story and my struggle for identity as an adopted child. Find out how I was able to find confidence and a spiritual awakening. I pray that this book will touch the lives of many who are searching, not only for their families, but also for a completeness that has been missing in their lives for maybe a long time.

Tell Me Universe

Tell me Universe
Who we are
Why have we come here
From afar?
What is our purpose?
Our reason for life?
And why do we endure
So much strife?

We're born into love
We're born into grace
And then life seems to give us
That slap in the face.
We want to escape
For we do not know
That we've chosen this life
From so long ago.

We planed all of it
Down to its core
Our soul knows its purpose
Though our minds say ~ No More!

If only we accept

And understand
That God is here for us
It's all part of the plan

To experience life
From A until Z
And come back again
If really need be
For if we are open
And willing to trust
All of life's Joy and Blessings
Will be placed upon us

For God wants us to be happy
Free of life's ills
But this is our choice
For we all have free wills

Chapter One

Looking back on my life, at the age of 55, I realize that it has been a world of growth, hardship, joy, love and pain. It has been a journey that I would never change, even though there were times I wanted to lock myself away from the world and end my existence.

Very often, as a child, there were times that I hated life, afraid to live fully. The weight of life often bore down on me like a heavy load, too much to carry. The overwhelming desperation of wanting to escape from the stress of the world and the pressures of life often made me just want to take an easy way out, and that easy way was to end it and be with love again in God's arms.

As a child gradually becoming aware of life, I had an uncommon longing for inner peace; and, like *few* people my age, I often felt the weight of the un-childlike world on my tiny shoulders. It was hard to breathe.

Happiness was of utmost importance to me, and I prayed for happiness—or what I thought it was—every day. I explicitly wished that I could live in my own perfect world, a place that somehow I could create for myself, a place where I would feel totally loved, complete, fearless, and whole. My small body, my child's mind, and my little heart yearned for something to fill an oversized—but unexplained—void that felt very real inside me.

At the time, I did not totally understand these feelings, but, looking back as I pen these words and feel the energy of who I was then, I realize now that, just before being that child, I had come from a place of ultimate love and peace (many religions name that state-of-being

Heaven); I can feel that place as I write; and in this moment, I consciously recognize, in a way that my young *soul* knew, but my young *mind* did not grasp, that the longing I felt as that sad child—was a Universal connection or desire within me to go back to that tranquil place, that place where I could feel complete.

In my own home—the place that two exceptionally loving people made for me—I was homesick. I longed to return to the prior place, of which I felt no longer a part, but which I remembered on a *sub-* or *super-*conscious level. In my *conscious* world, I felt lost and alone.

Just as a blind man trusts his seeing-eye-dog to guide him, I gradually learned to count on *my parents* to guide me along life's path. Trust in my parents was a wonderful thing, but taken to the extreme to which children often take such trust, it did not teach me how to stand on my own or to be responsible for my own life. Over time, this caused great pain.

My parents *transferred* some of the trust I had placed in them by telling me that *God* takes care of all people who give themselves over to Him. I liked hearing this. When they said it, a small part of me felt that I already knew it. I instantly loved the *idea* that God would protect and take care of me wherever I went. I really thought that God might be there, in the depths of my soul. On some level, my soul knew that I was loved by God. But, in the stark day-to-day reality of my physical world and in my mental torment, there I was, at the age of 5, feeling *alone*, even among people who loved me: I could not see God; I could not feel Him. I could not hear Him. *Where had he gone?!!!* How was I to find Him? Why had He, the Everything, abandoned me? I so desperately wanted to trust what my parents had told me—that He was there. But without proof, I found this so hard to do.

I think most of us hope that we can make a difference in this world, at least in some small way, during our lifetimes. As a child, I continually felt as if I never would.

You see, my parents smothered me with their love, protecting me and giving me all that they could. Included in that were lessons distinguishing right from wrong, lessons which were drilled into me in an endless array of variations, so that I would not forget. My parents taught me many things: manners, how to be kind to others, and how to be a lady. And since I was told far more often when I was doing *wrong* than right, I began to think I could *never* please them or be the perfect little girl they were looking for. I strived to do good in their eyes, hoping from the depth of my being to get their approval, hoping to feel like I made a difference, but even in the rare instances that I heard "You did a good job," there was always that "BUT, if you did this instead..." or "You could have done better."

It was April 1997 when my own daughter Holly called, down on her luck. She was 22 years old. She and her husband were living in Potsdam, NY, a small town not far from Canada; the two were trying to make a life for themselves by running their own business. Their business was not doing well. They had begun to acquire a large debt, and they tried working extra jobs to make ends meet. Holly was calling to ask my husband and me if she could come home and stay with us for a while. She did not know what else to do, and felt that she and her husband had done everything they could do to survive in Potsdam. She hoped that by coming home, they could start a new life for themselves, as long as we were willing to give them a chance.

Holly's call sent a myriad of emotions running though me. I wanted to help my daughter and her husband, but at the same time, I was taught by my parents that once a couple is married, they stayed together and did what they could on their own. "Tough Love" was my parents' belief, and they had taught me to believe that too. After all, I knew my parents' own difficult background, how hard they had had it, and what they expected of me. For years, I had watched them overcome obstacles in their lives, always keeping their emotions and feelings strictly to themselves. And, although in many ways I was a weak and shy little girl who smothered her true feelings until I was in my 40's, my parents' example of strength and Tough Love ultimately helped make me the strong person I am now.

I continually heard, as I grew up, how much joy and love a child could bring, and therefore I always envisioned myself as an eventual parent; I wanted some day to be one.

Until moments like this one in 1997—a phone call for help from afar and from across generations—I never knew what that really meant, or how intense your love could be for your own child. When I finally *was* blessed with children, I understood the words "a love that passes all understanding"—how a parent would die for her children, and pray at times for her children's pain to go away... always remembering that it is each child's choices and each child's destiny to fulfill his or her *own* joy and happiness; each child's life path was God's journey into His light.

I did not know my birth-parents; I was adopted. My mother and father, through the act of adopting, had found a space in their hearts to take into their lives more than one child. They wanted to give my brother and me a chance for a loving life, which otherwise, we might not have had.

Mom grew up on the west coast of Canada with two sisters and one brother. It was a very different kind of life. Her father owned a general store, and all of his children—including my mom—had to work there at some point during their lives, to help the family make ends meet. My mom's family was well-known by everyone in the community; the family reputation was important to their business. I often wondered if this could have been one of the reasons my mom did not like to share much of herself (word can travel fast in a small town). This is not to say that she did not have a wild side. There were times that she got into trouble, and I bet she often had to deal with how her actions appeared to her neighbors.

It was during World War II, my mom went to her friend Gladys's house for a party. Some of the soldiers who were stationed in Alaska were going to be there, and my mom's friend couldn't wait to introduce them to her. As the men arrived at Gladys's home, Gladys introduced them to my mom one at a time. One of the men, described later in family stories as "very attractive with dark black wavy hair, a beautiful smile, and loving eyes," slipped on the small entrance rug and fell flat on his face. He turned out to be the man that my mom would marry. She would tell my brother and me this story repeatedly as we grew up, saying that such was how our dad had fallen for her.

At 19 years old, a scared and young girl, my mom left home for the first time to travel across North America to New York... to marry a man she barely knew. The two lived in New Rochelle, north of New York City, for a stint in a small apartment with my dad's parents, and were lucky to save money to move to Levittown, Long Island into a beautiful new home. My dad's parents were also able to get a house in Levittown, just down the block. After a few years of having lived together in close quarters in New Rochelle, offspring and in-laws all knew that they got along pretty well.

Since my dad had been a photographer in the armed services, he was able to find a job working for a newspaper in Manhattan called *The Sun*. His workdays were very long, starting early in the morning.   Each day, he made the cumbersome trip into and out of 'the city'.

Life is never easy when you are young, married, and starting out on your own, and it certainly wasn't for my parents. But, they made many friends in the neighborhood that helped lift their spirits. They would enjoy taking turns at each other's homes, sharing the little wealth that they had by hosting an occasional dinner or party. The neighbors and my parents-to-be also belonged to the same Lutheran church, and two different couples from the area eventually became my brother's godparents and mine.

Years went by, and most of my parents' friends started having children. My parents wanted a child too, but they seemed to be having no luck. After seeing a doctor and having some tests, they found out that it was my father who was the cause of my mother's non-conception. Still wanting children, they decided to try and adopt. This young couple found that the process of adoption and intense questioning were more involved than they had ever expected. They hoped that it would not take long for the agency to find a child for them, but months and months went by. After three long *years* of waiting, the telephone finally rang, and the woman on the other end told this woman and this man that she felt that her organization had found the perfect little fifteen-month-old girl for them. My mom was so excited when she first saw me, she couldn't help but pick me up and hold me, even though she was told not to. The agency said that it did not want to cause any immediate attachments. Sadly, the man and the woman were not allowed to take me home and had to leave me behind. It was one of the hardest things that my parents ever had to do. Although I remember very little about this time in my life, I have relived this moment many times through my mother's and father's loving stories.

Finally the day came for me to come home. There was so much excitement in the neighborhood. Everyone knew how long my parents had been waiting. There were pictures galore, of course, since my dad was a photographer. Every moment of my life was captured, and there were lots of firsts to take since I did not walk or feed myself. My parents had much to teach me even though I wasn't a newborn. It wasn't long before they were blessed with another adopted child, this time a little boy who was two years younger than I was.

I was quickly taught how to get along with my adopted brother, and my mom made sure that I was involved in helping take care of him. He was a handful, between chewing through the bottom of the playpen, crawling out the window into the snow when he was suppose to be napping, getting up early before my mom was awake to try his hand in some cooking, and melting the plastic seat covers my mom had just replaced. And it didn't end there. One day, he was out and picked up a neighbor's milk bottle, which slipped out of his hands and broke. He found this so exciting that he proceeded to visit the rest of our neighbors' houses that morning, breaking their milk bottles too. My poor mother spent the rest of the day cleaning up the messes that he had left behind. Another time, little brother turned our water hose on and managed to lasso it into the window of our neighbor's house. These types of activities were more 'the rule' than 'the exception to the rule' for my younger sibling, growing up...and beyond.   He kept up this level and variety of mischievousness most of his young life, never giving my poor mom a break. She was lucky that I was such a well-behaved child because my brother and his shenanigans demanded a lot of her time, and kept my mother constantly on her toes.

My mother was a strong woman and had to handle a lot by herself since my father was rarely at home. My mother's friends could never understand how she did it.

With all the attention that my *brother* needed, and the strain that it put on my mother, *I* committed—at a young age—to trying to make my mother's life easier by doing everything *I* could *right*. As I mentioned, growing up, I often heard the words "You did a good job," along with its mandatory (seemingly conjoined) twin daggers "BUT, if you did this instead..." and (or) "you could have done better."   I remember one year in school working hard at one of the few subjects I was good at: "Art." We were drawing the human body that year, and for those of you who are artists, you know that the human body is one of the hardest things to draw and make life-like. I had done a drawing of a sailor, and I was so proud of it. I couldn't wait to get home and show my mom and dad. I showed it to my mom first, since my dad worked late and could see it later. As it turned out, my mom looked at the picture and told me how nice it was, and then proceeded to explain the different things I could do to make it look better, ending with, "well, you know it really is very good since I can't draw at all." Now, some people might say "well that wasn't so bad," but I wanted her to say four simple words: "What a good job." Instead I got a critique on how my picture could be improved.

I never did show the drawing to my dad, who was the artist in the family, in fear that he too would take apart my work. I felt down and depressed. I had thought that I could at *least draw.*

Maybe I was insecure. Where did that feeling come from? Even at that young age, it came from hearing over and over again "But" in most everything I did...and would do for years into my future. There was a guilt I would feel if I ever did anything wrong, for I wanted my parents to love me, treasure me, appreciate me, and most of all I wanted their compassion and attention.

One might ask, with all of the general fortune I experienced as a child, if I was spoiled. Well maybe I was a little, especially by my dad who would often enter the house from work bearing pretty and exciting gifts, but that didn't seem to displace or lessen the recurring— even growing—feeling and fear of abandonment that lived inside me, rearing its ugly head every step of the way, at even the hint of an opportunity to do so.

With it all, I knew, as I mentioned before, that my *parents* had never had it easy. I had heard their stories over and over again, like most of us do. Why did my parents tell me those stories so many times? Was it because they wanted me to respect them, live my life to their standards, or was it an underlying prayer for me to have a better life than they had?

Bouncing across the convoluted landscape of space-time, I too, have continually wanted my children to have a better life than mine. At one point, I wanted them to have a nice home, decent money, and as few hardships as possible.

I didn't know how much I was kidding myself at the time.

I believe now that we are our children's parents, and our job is to bring them up to be the best human beings they can be, but it is their own life. We may want them to have all the best that life can offer; we may want to protect them, and save them from ever being hurt. I have learned that we cannot do that. We can only guide them; for they have chosen to come to this planet to learn their own lessons and make a life for themselves, whether, it feels good or bad. A flood of awareness fills me: we did not choose our children; they chose us. Therefore, it is their destiny that must be fulfilled. We truly, as parents, don't have too much to say about that, for the play of their lives is all in God's hands. To me, it gradually has become clear: only God knows what is best for our children, because our children are really His children, children of the Universe; just as we ourselves are also His children.

~

Flash forward/back to April 1997. Holly on the phone. Time has stopped. The moment is boundless. Finally, my husband and I respond: We tell our daughter and her husband that they can come stay with us for a short while. Even though we deeply want them to make it on their own, I am not ready in this moment to let go and watch them fall on their faces. There would be a few adjustments for us all to make since Holly had been gone for a few years. Our house wasn't very big, and she and her husband would have to move whatever they had into her small bedroom. How would we all get along, I wondered? Would we fight all the time? What would happen to our privacy? I kept reflecting back on my life and how my mother had helped me when I was almost in

Holly's position. Yes, I knew it would be hard. But it was only for a short while, I reminded myself, and we would somehow get through it. God had already become a big part of my life, and had helped me cope with my divorce from my first husband who had beaten me. I had learned I could get though anything.

Good & Evil

Lucifer, Lucifer
The devil's your name?
You try and divert us?
It's all part of your game.
But your name really means
Light-Bearer--and so
We can see past the evil
And into your glow

For you are an angel
With a hell of a job
To show us life's balance
And help the poor slob
Who thinks that your evil
Is poised to destroy
All of life on this Earth
For each girl and boy

Yet God reins on high
And with Love shows his plan
He wants all off us
To truly understand
The difference between
What is bad... and what's good
For without Mr. Devil
All might be mis-understood

So I thank you Lucifer
For the balance you give
So I can appreciate
God's light, love… and live
For without all life's contrasts
For me to perceive
I might not fully appreciate
All God's gifts I receive

Chapter Two

Holly said that she would come home by herself at first. Her husband, Bill, whom I admired for all that he was doing, was closing up the store and finalizing things with their business. I told my daughter that her dad and I would allow the two of them to stay with us for a few months until they could get back on their feet and find their own place to live.

When Holly arrived home, she was drained and tired, but beneath her fatigued surface radiated an unmistakable hope and a promise for a better life. Holly settled in and started right away putting out applications for a new job and going to interviews. Bill arrived on the scene about a month later and also started the job search. I was happy to see that they were both serious about getting work, saving money, and doing what they could do to get back on their feet. I wasn't going to put up with any procrastination.

Holly landed a job right away at a local greeting card store. I was so happy for her, since her confidence had grown weak from looking for extra work up in Potsdam, which she couldn't find despite her continuous efforts. I was hoping that her new job down here would lift her spirits, but for some reason, she was down in the dumps and not feeling well. This surprised me, and although I was concerned, I chalked it up to the life changes and stress that she had just been through.

I was glad that everyone was getting along so well in our home: with one bathroom and five people living together, we all tried to be as accommodating as possible. We were proud that even our son, Nick, who was 19 years old and 3 years younger than Holly, extended himself and made things easier on his sister and her husband. Staying out of each other's way was not an easy task for any of us, and it was even more difficult to mind our own business. The living quarters were so close that anything anyone said could be heard in any room.

One day, while trying to mind my P's and Q's, I overheard Holly and Bill arguing in her bedroom. She hadn't been feeling well for some time now and he was trying to force her to take some new herbs that he had bought. Unfortunately, their medical insurance hadn't kicked in yet, and they were doing whatever they could do to avoid the doctor. Holly was crying; she could not get the herbs down, and he was being insistent. She kept yelling, "I can't swallow them, I can't!" She was getting hysterical and I couldn't take it anymore; I had to go in and see what was wrong.

I knew that it was really none of my business, but something inside was telling me that this was serious. I had learned to pay attention to my intuition over the years and the feeling of dread was very strong.

I believe that our intuition is one of our main connections to Spirit. I am not saying that we should walk around feeling fearful of everything; only that our inner feelings are there for a reason, to protect us if necessary and even to let us know when something important is coming our way. God has given us these feelings for a reason. It is one of the ways he keeps in touch with us and guides us through our everyday lives. All we have to do is practice breathing, living in the moment, and recognizing when something feels right or wrong. With practice, I have learned to trust my inner feelings over the years. When I feel something now, I ask myself if it is a loving thought and for everyone's higher good; if the answer is "yes," I never go wrong.

I walked into my daughter's room with a sick feeling inside, looked at the kids, and asked them what the hell was going on. Holly's husband looked at me and said "She has to take these herbs if she wants to get better and she won't take them." Holly looked at me with tears in her eyes and said, "I can't mom, I just can't." Her expression cut right through me. I knew my daughter would take the herbs if she could. I asked her what she was feeling, and she said that it felt like there was no room in her stomach even to swallow water and that her chest and back hurt. How long has this been going on, I asked? A few weeks, she said.

"I don't understand what the problem is," I replied, "but even though you have no medical coverage, we should go to the doctor to try and find out why you're feeling this way." I told them that I would pay for any expenses incurred; at this point it didn't matter to me. I was determined to fix whatever was wrong.

Although Holly was married, I still was her mom and believed that there was going to be a way that I could protect her from everything. I have learned since then that such is not necessarily the case—nor necessarily even a *good* thing.

The three of us loaded into the car and went to our local family doctor, who did not take appointments. He examined Holly and told us that he wanted her to see a gynecologist and have a sonogram performed right away. Concerned, we left his office and went straight to the medical center around the corner; they took her right in. What had the doctor seen to make him feel that there was a need for all of this right away, we thought, as Bill and I patiently waited in the waiting room, praying that everything was all right.

They finally called us into the back room to speak to us. It had only been about 20 minutes, but it felt like hours. They said that the sonogram pictures showed that Holly had a fifteen-inch ovarian cyst. I couldn't believe my ears. My mind couldn't fathom what the doctor had said. "How big did you say it was?," I asked again. "Fifteen inches," said the doctor repeating herself, "and we have never seen one this large. It goes from her lower abdomen all the way up to her rib cage." I was in shock! What could we do? We knew we first had to figure out how to handle this situation money-wise. So with no further appointment, we went home.

There was no doubt that we needed to move quickly; the doctor had said the cyst should come out as soon as possible, and Holly was getting worse every day. She and her husband were very young and neither of them knew facilities in the area, so I told them about a place that would charge according to their salary. I hoped that this would help them afford whatever medical expenses were to come. They got the soonest appointment they could, telling the office staff that it was an emergency. When the doctors there saw the size of the cyst, they also could not believe it. We were stunned when they told her to go home and come back in a week. I was overwhelmed with what was happening and upset. What were the doctors thinking? "She needs an operation and right away," I thought.

Within that week, I read everything I could get my hands on about ovarian cysts. I found that it was rare to have one that size, although there had been larger ones reported. I also felt sick to learn that there was a chance that a cyst or tumor that size could burst inside the patient, sending toxins throughout their body. I tossed and turned at night worrying that something terrible could happen to my daughter. A feeling of helplessness came over me, and every moment I could, I prayed for God to help us. I never cared before about my family's medical history, but now it was important. I needed to find some resource, I needed someone to help us and give us some answers.

~

Within a day or two after being seen by those first doctors, Holly got even worse. I pushed Bill to handle as much as possible on his own and guided him through every step since I couldn't bear to sit idle. I told him to call the health center again, insisting that they set her up for surgery. When they told him that they would get back to him, I was livid. What, were they crazy?!! We needed to do something right away. Holly was in severe pain and crying! We waited that morning for the health center to call back, which they never did; I was at my wits' end. I told Holly and her husband that we were not waiting anymore, and we were going to the emergency room of our local hospital.

With the long hours that my husband worked, I was alone to handle this situation. I called him and told him that I was taking his daughter to Emergency and we would deal with whatever was going to happen.

I had no idea at the time what we were in for that day, but things had become so bad for my daughter, I knew that we needed help. I had to trust that whatever was to come, we would deal with it, and that it was going to be all right. I believe that God never gives you more than you can handle, even though there have been times in my life that I have felt I was at my breaking point. I had to remember during those times that no matter how hopeless a situation might seem, things always somehow work out. They say we are always growing in our lives, but if you really think about your own spiritual growth, isn't it the times that are the hardest when you grow the most? These are our spiritual learning lessons that usually help make our inner light glow. I am reminded of the song from Annie "[The Sun'll Come Out] Tomorrow." Somehow God always makes the sun come out, so we need to stop worrying so much, and Let Go, and let God.

When we got to the emergency room at Huntington Hospital, I called my mother, told her why we were at the hospital, and asked her if she could come and assist me if possible. I knew that Holly's husband was going to have to leave soon, since it was to be the first day on his new job. I was praying that I could stay with Holly for as long as she needed me, but I had 40 students waiting for me that afternoon—they were waiting for me to teach them their last dance class of the term, preparing them for their dress rehearsal that was two days away. I wanted to cry. I had no one to help me with my classes, especially at this last minute, and I didn't want to leave my daughter. DEAR GOD, I cried, "why are you doing this?"

~

The hospital wanted to contact the health center; they insisted on speaking to someone who could fill them in on Holly's case, even though we had told them repeatedly what had gone on during the past few weeks. Hours went by before the emergency doctor finally reached someone at the health center who could give them some answers. No one was telling us what was happening, and we wondered why it was taking so long to get Holly some help. Finally, we found out that the health center would not agree to the operation.

Thank God for the emergency room doctor who fought with them to get her into surgery.

My mom was able to arrive at the hospital in time for me to explain what was happening, and for me to leave for my dance classes. It took everything in my power to walk out of the hospital that day, leaving my mother and daughter behind before my daughter had even gone into surgery.

I could barley teach my classes; I was too busy praying that everything would go well. My only saving grace was that I knew she was in God's hands.

> *I was 12 years old the first time that I had truly felt God's love. I had been told growing up that I should believe he was up there watching me. I have learned over the years that there is a difference between believing and knowing.*

~

My father's father died before I was two. He barely had the chance to get to know me. I don't remember him at all, but to this day, I have a picture that he painted for me hanging in my home. His wife was a very prim and proper lady, always dressed to the nines. I can remember my grandma's house, filled with things that she and grandpa had collected in their travels around the world while he was in the Service. One room in particular scared me, with all its weird masks. When my brother and I got the chance to stay overnight, we would pray that we wouldn't have to sleep in that room. I knew of the devil; and the scary masks made me feel that He was a little too close by. The fear of that room was only one of the *many* evil things that I felt lurking around me as I grew up.

The mind is a very powerful thing, and I don't believe that evil lurks everywhere. Besides, the word "Lucifer" means "Light-Bearer." Maybe this angel's real job is to show us the dark side of things so that we can see the positive and negative for ourselves. It is up to us to find the positive in what we might think the negative is. Everyone's perception of reality is different. If you think about it, we really do create our own reality. There was a story I heard once of two men who climb up a mountain as the wind begins to blow. Once they reach the top, one man is afraid and can't imagine how he will ever get down the mountain if he doesn't blow off of it first. The other man stretches out his arms to the beauty of nature and embraces it enjoying the moment to its fullest. How do we destroy or enjoy the moments of our lives?

My grandmother had a lot of love in her heart and would always try to make our visits with each other special. One of the things we especially enjoyed was baking with her, and of course, eating all the goodies that we co-created.

As my brother and I grew older, it looked to me like he was having a lot of fun, even though he was getting into lots of trouble. There were times that my brother talked me into doing a few things that I shouldn't have done.

We would take small metal pellets used in a pellet gun and smash them with a hammer. When we smashed them (to this day, I can't remember exactly where we got the pellets—probably one of my brother's friends), they would flatten out like a penny and were perfect for putting into candy machines instead of a penny. I knew that doing this was wrong, but what kid can resist a little candy and we only used a few slugs at a time. Although I ·tried to be the perfect little girl, I had my moments of getting into trouble. I can remember one time wanting so badly to see my boyfriend, I disregarded my parents' clear wishes. I was in love and no one was going to stop me from seeing him. My mother and father did not want me spending that much time with any boy, since I was only 15 years old. The restrictive attitude of my parents was a problem for Joe and me. But not an insurmountable one: Joe was very inventive and he made a telephone that would tap out the phone numbers, kind of like Morse code. He put it in a cigar box and hooked it up to the telephone line in my parent's room and slipped it under their wall and into my room by my bed. This way, I could talk to Joe all night. When my parents found out, they were livid. They didn't know what to say to me and they would often blame my friends for leading me down the wrong path. I even got arrested one night by the police, walking the streets at 2:00 in the morning to get to Joe's house to see him. I certainly wasn't always that perfect little girl, and when I got into trouble my mom would often say things like; "Why did you do that! Don't you love me?" Or, "You wouldn't have done that if you really loved me!"

It wasn't just church that tried to drill the fear of God into me by saying that if you truly loved God, and did what He wanted you to do, then He would love you in return. I also learned that at home.

My family life often seemed pretty normal. However, there were secrets kept in the closet, and since my brother and I had been so young when we were adopted, my parents felt no need to tell us that the people with whom we were living, and all the family members that we knew, were not our true relatives. I spent all of my childhood not knowing the truth.

I wanted to know the truth, and I wanted to know it then. There are many things we want in life that are beyond the materialistic that just don't seem to happen. What do we do when they don't happen? We often get upset and annoyed. I have gradually evolved to discover that maybe we should stop for a moment and ask ourselves if we are truly ready for these desired events to occur. Maybe the reason something isn't happening is because we are blocking it for some reason, or maybe we should be thinking—even knowing—that it will happen in God's time, for He is the one who truly knows when we are ready.

At times, as a growing little child, I had been feeling a loss or distance from my family, sort of like something was *missing*, but I could not put my finger on what it was. One specific memory would recur in my mind and I would wonder if this was truly a memory or my imagination. I could recall myself as a toddler, maybe around 8 months old, so small that I could not walk yet. I would be sitting on a small blanket with an adult. A brick building was nearby, and I was watching other children playing at the distant playground. I did not know what significance to attach to this recurring vision and the strange undefined intuition that seemed linked to it, haunting me in a persistent yet unthreatening way as I gradually grew. It wasn't until an unexpected conversation with my mother later, when I was 11, that this memory made sense to me.

~

Our family soon moved again, this time out a little further east to Huntington, in Suffolk County. This house was much bigger than the last, and I started school, taking the bus in second grade. Although I was a good child in school, and I tried very hard, my teachers were concerned about the difficulties that I was having with my schoolwork. After many conferences, my teachers, parents, and the board decided without acknowledging my feelings that I should be left back. I am sure that they all thought they were helping me, but at seven years old, I had already developed a severe lack of confidence and I feared that their decision might not be the best.

My fears were confirmed when the following year came. I felt totally out of place. All my friends were now a grade ahead of me, and I felt that they certainly did not have to be told that I was not smart enough to keep up with them. Because of this, my relationships with the few friends I did have totally changed, and I had to begin to make new relationships. My schoolwork didn't improve either, and I started to feel angry about what had been done to me. Where was the love of my parents? Didn't they care about my feelings? Why didn't they ask me what I wanted before doing this to me? I feel society sometimes puts too much emphasis on intelligence. Who is to say that one child is smarter than the next? When are we going to realize that every child has a special place in this world and is in that place for a special reason?

Over the next few years I was forced to sit in the front of the classroom. My teachers thought that this would help me be more involved in what was going on. I didn't want to sit in the front since I already felt like a freak, felt uncomfortable, and hated answering questions and having people stare at me, which turned out to be most of the time. My depression got so bad at times that even if I thought I knew the answer to a question I would not answer, fearing the embarrassment of it all.

One of my teachers got so angry trying to force me to give an answer to a question that he put his foot up on my desk and proceeded to push the desk into my stomach, hoping that he could make me talk. I would not give him an answer; I'd rather feel the pain. My fear of being wrong outweighed the embarrassment of the situation.

I began to hate school, yet I was hardly ever absent. I strived to get the award of no absences during the year 'cause I believed I was a stupid child and figured this was one thing I could do right. I went to school no matter how I felt, even if I was so sick I could hardly keep my eyes open. My parents never knew how bad I was feeling at times, or the depth of what I was going though inside.

I was not fully aware of the crippling feeling of abandonment that was growing within me; maybe that is why I wanted to be liked by everyone, to be the perfect friend and make them all happy—Oh, if it were only possible. I had hoped it could be. I lived a large part of my life trying to be liked by everyone, but I was only tormented by the fear and indecision that living with such an unattainable goal brought. I hated conflict, and would avoid it like The Plague, to the point of lying if need be.

Lying became a problem for a while because I wanted so much to be liked and accepted by people. Sometimes I would make up some silly little story to try and get others to notice me, but found that one lie would lead to the next. I would get so caught up in the stories that I was telling, that I began to believe them myself. In the beginning, I told tiny lies to gain admiration, like telling people I had received a beautiful new dress, which I didn't really receive. Later, as a teenager, the lies were a little bigger. At one point, I convinced my friends that I was a singer in my boyfriend's band.

I wanted to be popular at all costs. My pattern of lying was not only unhealthy, but it was also ineffective for me: nothing changed in my life, and I tossed myself into a fantasy world of untruths. Fantasy was a simple concept for me since I did not like the real world, and I hoped to live in a fantasy every day. Fantasy was a safe way for me to avoid the useless person that I thought I was and a way out of exposing my true self to others.

> *My self-worth had been pushed to the limit. I felt that the person I was, was built upon what I could or couldn't do. What about the God within me? I did not know of Him at the time. My understanding of the truth that we are all part of God was not a part of my life yet.*

Amidst my secret struggling with life, struggling which far exceeded the boundaries of school, my mom on occasion sought to help me overcome my less secret struggles with schoolwork. She offered to help me study for tests, and I let her, but for some reason, I always found it hard to remember what I had read. She thought that if I began reading out loud to her from the book that I was assigned to study, this practice would help me better remember the words that I was reading. This would also give her the chance to hear aloud and understand the material I was required to study; this exercise enabled her to ask me a few questions from the passages. She prayed that this process would be a perfect solution to the problem that I was having. In reality, it worked out differently: I made the attempt one time to read out loud to her three or four pages from a book; when she went to ask me her questions I could not answer one. She could not understand why I was having so much trouble, and she would painfully hound me for an answer. That only made me more afraid of her, and from the core of my being, I pulled away from this process. After much frustration on her part, one day she asked me why I was having a problem. I simply told her that I hated what I was reading and that it was hard for me to concentrate, especially on a subject that I didn't like. What she didn't know—and what I sometimes chose not to recognize—was that, while reading aloud, my mind could go someplace else, someplace far, far away from the deafening pain deep inside me.

"Casper the Friendly Ghost" was one of my favorite television shows and I would pretend that Casper would be with me wherever I went. I loved the idea of a friendly ghost and He kept me company. I imagined him sitting next to me in school and would have private little conversations with him in my mind. This seemed fine since he was a Ghost and could hear and know everything I was thinking without anyone else knowing he was there. He held my hand during my tests and was my friend when I felt completely alone. I knew that it was a bit odd to have a friend like him, but he gave me the comfort and love I so desperately needed. I would often fail a subject or two every semester except the last. I am sure my teachers just gave me a passing grade because they knew I had little confidence, had been left back before, and they didn't have the heart to fail me.

My mom, who was always trying to do the right thing by helping me, was concerned one year that I would fail Social Studies. She went to the school one day to speak to my teacher and asked him if there was some kind of project that I could do to help improve my grade. She told him that none of this would matter to me in my future when I was a wife and a mother having children. Although I was thankful for her help, I was devastated to think that maybe all that I could do in my life was be a wife, mother, and to have children. Wasn't my life worth more than just getting married and having children and doing for *others*? Didn't I have some *personal* self-worth?

The teacher told my mother that I could build the Capitol Building. My father showed me how to make it out of toothpicks, which gave me a good grade, and I passed that year. But at what expense to my personality and confidence?

My dad would bring home candy and toys to try and make up for his absence, since he had to work such long hours. He wished he could spend more time with us, so weekends were very important to him. He would often come home just before I went to bed during the week, so it was up to my mother to do her best to give me the confidence I needed. She would often tell me how wonderful my work was, but the effect of her words was lost when the inevitable "But" invariably emerged. I knew that my mom loved me, and I tried to do the best that I could to make her proud.

I prayed that I could feel comfortable enough to communicate all the fears within me, but there wasn't much communication in our family, and I was afraid to disappoint my mother or make her mad. I knew very well that she could get mad, for I would often lay in bed at night listening to my mom and dad yell at each other. Holding all of these emotions inside made me a sad and very lonely girl. I continued to feel separated from the world.

This feeling of separation from the world has happened to me a few times in my life. I used to feel that at every moment some kind of growth should be occurring and that if you were idle or your life didn't seem to be moving forward, this was a bad thing. I believe now that when things in life seem to be in a holding pattern, it doesn't mean that inner growth is not occurring, all it means is that it is a time for reflection, which although we may not believe it, can be a good thing. Moments like these can bring much needed balance, focus, and inner truth into our lives.

In sixth grade, a miracle occurred when the school nurse checked my eyesight and found that I desperately needed glasses. I had been checked every year prior and yet, for some reason, my poor vision was not found. The look of shock on my mother's face when I put my first pair of new glasses on and could read the clock above the kitchen refrigerator was amazing. The clock was large with big numbers, and she was surprised, to say the least, that I had never been able to read it. I did not think anything of my vision problem; I was near-sighted, and just thought that everyone else saw the same as me. The miracle was that my schoolwork improved some, and I was finally able to read from the blackboard that I hadn't been able to for years.

I hated reading all the way up to sixth grade even though Mrs. Healy, the librarian, tried to help me by filling my arms with fiction books. One time, she saw me putting a bunch of books that she had picked out for me, back on the shelf as I was leaving the library. Taking me aside, she asked me why I didn't want the books, and I reluctantly told her that I didn't like to read. She said that she was sure she could find something that would interest me. She took me around the library asking me if I liked this kind of book or that. It wasn't until she reached the non-fiction section that a few books sparked my interest. Most of the kids in my class had enjoyed reading fiction and she was surprised to find that non-fiction books were more my speed. It was Mrs. Healy's love and kindness that got me interested in reading and opened a door to the world of non-fiction. My dad also helped me acquire a joy for reading by handing me a book one day by Edgar Alan Poe. I responded by reading everything he ever wrote. For the first time in my life, the wonder of reading meant something to me. Reading has since enhanced my life in so many ways, and the knowledge that I have gained has changed who I am.

~

It was during this time period that my mom, who was doing laundry one day, called my brother and me into her bedroom. As we sat on her bed watching her fold clothes, she told us how much she loved us, and that all of her life she had longed to have children. She explained how some mothers just become pregnant, and in nine months have a baby. She said that she loved us so much, that she was willing to wait 3 years to have us. That's when she told my brother and me that we were adopted. To this day, I have no idea how my brother handled that information. I was shocked that she had kept this a secret for so long. My brother was 9 and I was

11. Why hadn't she told us sooner? My breath was missing; I was in disbelief.

When I finally calmed down, I realized that the way that my mom had told us was really beautiful. I couldn't imagine how anyone could love as much as she did. I certainly knew I was blessed to have her and my dad. However, in the back of my mind during those early years of my life, I did increasingly begin to wonder where I might have come from, why I was given up, and who my real family was.

All of this new information made my mind spin and sat heavy on my heart. Just when I was beginning to do better in school, I was pulled down again by all of this information, and now felt I owed my mother and father more for saving me from a life of horror and sadness. Why was life such a roller coaster ride? I wanted to get off! I couldn't understand the point of it all, or what the reason was for us all to be here.

Our family continued going to church and joined a Lutheran church in Huntington. I sang in the choir and took confirmation classes, but wasn't too fond of church. The words to the songs and the hope of God loving you if you were a good person brought some peace into my life, but I wondered if God was really all-loving like people said he was. If so, why wouldn't you be forgiven if you sinned? I was taught that if you sinned and did not repent you would go to hell. What if you made one mistake and didn't know you sinned? Would you be forgiven? Where was His almighty love that I had heard so much about? I knew how strong my own father's love was for me, so why would God ever deny me His love? Because of this concern, the fear of death grew stronger within me during those years. I was scared to death that

I would screw up somehow and would end up in hell for eternity.

~

I finally got to see God's love when I went to Lutheran camp for the summer. I was 12 years old.   It was my first chance away from my family and a time for me to reflect. I loved the woods and I had gone off by myself to write letters to my loved ones. While sitting by a stream, I looked up at the beautiful sights of nature, and in that instant something touched my heart. A feeling of overwhelming joy came into me and I knew that there was no way the world's perfection could exist without God. Everything was just too exquisite in its wholeness and beauty, and I felt it could not be complete without His wonderment and Love.

God's power was proven to me again that summer when a close friend of mine, Diane, was crying. She had just recently lost her dog, and was overwhelmed with sadness because there was another dog on the campgrounds that looked just like hers and kept reminding her of her loss. She ran up to her cabin in tears. I felt helpless. I wished there were something I could do. But what could I do to cheer her up, I thought, since in my heart I knew that she was a much better person than I. I called upon God for guidance. I prayed every inch of the way to the cabin for the Lord to help me find the words to make her feel better and make everything all right. I don't remember the exact words I said, but I know that the words that I spoke came from God through me, and I was able to help her instantly, with Divine guidance, in my small way. These events were my first real experiences and proof, that I was not alone in this world, that there is always someone there to guide you, if only you ask.

My dad, who was able to get quite a bit of time off in the summer, loved to camp and so did my brother and I. We spent weeks camping even though my mother hated it. We would travel across New York State and into the Adirondack Mountains going from one campsite to the next for almost a month. It was during this time period that I made my first connection to Spirit by hearing its/their words. I did not know this at the time and just felt it was another occasion where my mind and creative imagination were running wild.

I was walking on the stones along the shore of a lake, among the beautifully shaped driftwood, looking out at an island off-shore when these beautiful words came into my mind:

The sky is bright, the heavens glow,

The time is right, so I must go.

Down to the shore, where I can see,

The sunlit lake, and can be free.

My heart is filled with happiness,

As I walk on the shore with carefree-ness.

The beautiful trees bow with grace,

And the island seems like an endless place,

To build a house and to be free,

From ties with all, except the sea.

I wrote them down, but it wasn't until I was older that I discovered that this awareness and process would be an important way for me to connect to Spirit.

My dad was a very friendly person and would often rally the kids in the campgrounds together by planning scavenger hunts. I just loved this, and since I was shy, I found it a nice way to meet new people. I enjoyed taking walks in the woods with my dad, looking at the sights of nature while he took rolls of pictures. He was an avid reader who remembered all he read, and knew the name of every fascinating thing in the forest. During our walks I learned so much, and the connection that I lacked with my mom was filled, to an extent, by my Dad's attention. Because of these experiences, to this day I feel a great connection to spirit through nature.

My dad was a kind man and had so much love for others in his heart. Anyone who met him fell in love with his smile and loving nature. He would often tease my friends and make them laugh. He loved to eat and often would attempt some kind of gourmet dinner that he would serve to the family. I thought he would make the perfect Santa Claus, and once in a while, he would entertain the children in just such a persona at a church event.

I escaped from my problems whenever possible, by dancing around my living room to whatever music I could find. "Hey Little Cobra" by the Rip Cords was one of my first records, and I played it until it almost wore out. It was obvious to my parents that I liked to dance. I had the music on and was moving around the room almost every day. Seeing how much I loved dancing, and despite their uncertain financial situation, my parents asked me if I would like to try some dance lessons. I was thrilled! Finally, it was something that I felt I could do, and I caught onto the steps very fast. This wonderful experience was short-lived when the teacher put me in front of the class to help her lead all of the other kids. Even though this was something I could do, I certainly did not want to be in the front of the class; besides, I was bored with the steps. My teacher spoke to my parents about private lessons; however, they were too expensive, and at the end of the year, I decided to drop out of the teacher's class.

All of the ups and downs that I experienced in my early childhood brought me much happiness and pain. Although I was still lacking a lot of confidence, I had the support of my parents most of the time. They were always there when there was something important going on in my life. I never wanted to disappoint them. I wanted them to love me, but I was afraid that I would never live up to their standards of me. I was afraid not to honor them, for this was one of His commandments, and I could go to hell. So I tried to be strong, and the good little girl; I didn't want to ruffle anyone's feathers.

My mom was the strongest one in the family. There was much she had to handle alone, with my father's long hours at work and his going in and out of the city. We went through many hard times with the lay-offs that occurred by the merging of different newspapers which he worked for. These changes in the name of my father's employer, which I didn't fully understand, left him out of work sometimes for months. The newspaper he worked for called THE SUN became the *Telegram and Sun, the World Telegram and Sun,* and *the World Journal Tribune.*

Things were always hush-hush in our house when another such change was in progress. No one on the outside was ever allowed to know how hard things were for us, and there was never any talk even *within* the family of our financial situation. "Children should be seen and not heard," was my grandmother's motto and it became my parent's too whenever we asked a question.

~

My parents were survivors. They had come so far in their lives, and I knew I had also made it though tremendous turmoil. My mom would say, "You are a Higgins; you can handle anything that comes your way, we are survivors." I wasn't sure if I could handle anything that came my way, but I knew I was a survivor.

Unexpected Angels

Unexpected Angels
Unexpected turns
Leading us through life
Just for us to learn

Power and believing
What is in your heart
Never really knowing
That we are all a part

Of His gentle Spirit
Of His loving grace
Of His every being
We should all embrace

The power that's within us
The power of our soul
The moments that we waste
Can make life so very cold

So find the truth inside you
Find the love within

Find the path that leads you
Through life with a grin

Perpetuate the knowledge
That only your soul knows
Allow it to renew you
For this is the path you chose

Believe in your tomorrows
And never do forget
That life is to be cherished
Not to have regrets

Chapter Three

My mother was sitting in the hospital waiting room when I got there. She looked exhausted, but something in my mom's face immediately told me that my daughter had come out of the surgery okay. My husband Bob was with me this time.

Mother told us slowly that the surgery had gone well and that the doctor had said it was one of the biggest benign tumors that he had ever seen. My mom was absolutely exhausted, and I thanked her for everything that she had done during these past few trying hours. I thanked her for being with Holly when her father and I were unable to be there. Mom went home to rest.

Bob and I took the elevator up to see our daughter: she was very groggy from the operation. But it was still her. We held her hand. We sat with her for a while. We had a few words. We nonverbally enveloped her with our deepest love. It wasn't until the next day, when we returned, that Holly filled us in on the details about her operation.

My daughter told us the incredible story of how she and her grandmother had to make a big decision on what to do before the surgery. The doctor had given them two options: one was to remove the whole cyst by cutting Holly from her groin all the way up to her chest. The good thing about this option was that the whole tumor could be removed intact; the bad part was that this procedure could severely threaten her ability to have children in the future. Holly was only 21 years old. The second option that the doctors offered was: to cut my daughter from the same spot up to merely her belly button, and drain the fluid in the tumor before removing it, thereby making it possible to extract the tumor through a smaller, less disruptive, incision. I imagined the two women dearest to me, hours before, consulting with each other in a fog of uncertainty—following only their own instincts and those of each other. Ultimately, they opted for the second option: the smaller cut.

In Holly's hospital room, as I learned these details, I also learned that the preliminary indications were that the chosen strategy had succeeded. The tumor indeed was drained and some of Holly's organs had been *lifted out* and held by the nurses so that the doctor could see clearly what he was doing. The tumor had been entwined around most of my daughter's major abdominal organs. The doctor was forced to remove one ovary and one fallopian tube, but he told my daughter that she should still be able to have children.

Within two days, Holly was doing much better. The hospital released her in time to see the dance recital, the performance for which other young people had been preparing passionately under my mentorship. (Holly, literally following in some of my own footsteps, had been dancing since she was a little girl; she loved dancing. And she was always involved in helping me with the recitals.) Dancing was not only my passion, but it was also my daughter's, and she never wanted to miss one recital. She had been looking forward to this particular event all year.

The next few days, Holly continued to recover, but she found it very hard to move around. Due to her organs' temporary displacement during the operation, my daughter said that it felt like her internal body parts were now sloshing around in the empty space that currently existed where the large cyst had been removed.

For quite a while, movement bothered Holly, especially if she was in a car when it hit a bump.

I couldn't believe all that my daughter had been through in the last few days—and at such a young age. I was relieved that my mom had said it was the largest benign tumor the doctor had ever seen. However, the biopsy results were not in yet, and although I wanted to think positively, I knew that my mind would not rest until the results were in.

Holly had lost about *20* pounds in 3 days, and although she looked much better, she was thin and a little frail. My daughter didn't let her physical trauma slow her down much though, and within a month, she was back at work!

We didn't talk much at that time, the two of us, about her personal feelings and all that she had been through. It wasn't until much later that Holly told me how spiritually altering the whole experience was, and how she had found inner strength that she never thought she had. In subsequent conversations with my daughter, I found that Holly's spiritual searching (and finding) resonated with something deep inside myself. I too was a person who was not fully aware of the universal strength that perpetually supported me—and like Holly, I had found that strength hidden within myself, and bathing me from above, at times I least expected. As I continued to question God's love, myself, my destiny and my purpose in life... the answers— and the *hope* that I so desperately needed — revealed themselves to me gradually, the way that the sun gradually emerges from beneath the darkest clouds.

As a child, I had lots of Questions, but it was a sin to ask too many. You would be told that the Bible was truth, and anything against it or the church was a sin. Of course, I did not want to sin. The fear of even asking these kinds of questions was always on my mind. So there was no one to talk to about what I was feeling and what I was thinking. Most of the questions I had were about God's infinite love. I found it impossible to believe that a true loving God should be feared. Something inside of me told me this was not my truth or God's.

I was 15 years old and in my last year at Burr's Lane Junior High School, when my friends asked me to go with them to a dance. The dance was held at Candlewood Junior High School—my friend's school— nearby. We had a wonderful time dancing together and the end of the evening was drawing near. I had prayed for a boy to ask me to dance, but felt that such an outcome was unlikely since I saw myself as a shy and ugly little girl. I was just about to give up hope when a cute young guy with long, wavy blond hair came over and asked me to join him on the dance floor. It was the first time that any guy had really noticed me and shown me some attention. I was not popular in school and most of my friends already had boyfriends. I fell in love for the first time that night with this young man named Joe. I was thrilled to have him look my way, and we became great friends, since we had so much in common. Our time together was usually spent inventing and creating Joe's wonderful ideas, which I enjoyed. He was my first real boyfriend. He made me feel special, and I felt that I was truly in love with him, a feeling with which at the time, I was not very familiar. Our relationship grew very strong and I wanted to be with Joe every chance I got. Our parents tried to keep us on track with what they thought the more important things in life were: school, church, and family life. I think they were concerned about how involved Joe and I were getting with each other.

My parents were right to be concerned, because after two years of being together, Joe and I made love to each other for the first time. It was rather interesting though because we had to buy a book from a drugstore to read about what we were supposed to do. We loved each other so much, that the learning process just enhanced our love-making experience. I will never forget how gentle and kind he was or regret him being the first guy I was with. I know my parents would not have approved of this if they knew. We were young, and sex as a teenager, without marriage, was a big no-no.

I had a lot of ups and downs with friendships: given my history of being left back, sometimes feeling isolated at school, and having had friends move away. My heart was repeatedly broken. Near the end of elementary school, I met a girl named Jeanine through a mutual friend, one of my few at the time. It was slow-going at first, but in a short time, we were by each others' side whenever possible. The two of us clung together like Siamese twins and needed each other in so many ways: she was an only child, and I had just my brother. We were both in love, so there was much to share, and we did so sometimes by buying a bag of candy and watching a crazy movie to lift our spirits whenever one (or both) of us felt down. I can remember making a clubhouse out of a big box that we found on the side of the road. It seemed like the longer we knew each other, the more confidences we would share and the more support we were able to give to each other. Jeanine, it turns out, would be with me not only during awkward adolescence, but also though my father's illness, his death, and my first marriage. I was able to be by her side when her mother died and when she went through her divorce. As I write this, almost 40 years have passed since Jeanine and I first met, and we are still remarkably close. The hopes and dreams and life events we've shared are too numerable to mention, but our love for each other has stayed strong and has made a permanent mark on my soul. To this day, Jeanine has been the sister that I never had, and I have learned from her what a true friend really is. It is a blessing when you find a true friend who knows how to give unconditional love.

The needs of a young adult do change, and my parents expected me to handle those needs myself. They were not able to hand me money whenever I wanted it, and I was expected to work for anything extra that I needed. My first job was working in the local library as a 'page' where the staff was nice enough to give me a variety of things to do like filing and checking out books, making posters, and reading to the children during story hour. I enjoyed the job. I met some very nice people and tried to be a conscientious worker. When they would say I did a good job, it meant the world to me. I didn't realize at the time the strength and confidence that I was trying so hard to build with this first employment experience after years of hurt and mistrust growing up.

I still didn't have much of a relationship with God, but I had found the love that I was searching for through my relationship with Joe. After time, that relationship grew very intense but he now was playing in a band, and the girls were all over him. This did not make me happy, and I found that even if you think things are perfect, life can unexpectedly pull the carpet right out from under you.

Why does this happen? Why does life sometimes feel like it's built on a foundation of quicksand?

Maybe God finds that we are sitting idle for too long and wants to kick us in the ass—so to speak—to get us moving. Maybe the kind of things that we are praying for are really coming true, but in a different way than we had planned. Maybe there are some learning lessons that we need to learn before what we want is just handed to us. One way or the other, when our dreams do finally come true, and when we have gone through all the ups and downs of life, I am sure that God hopes that we will appreciate His wonderment and the gifts that He has given us.

Desperation & Despair or Love & Peace

Oh Lord ~
It hurts so bad; the desperation that I feel within me is so hard to bear.
I sense my mind's confusion; my heart is beating fast; and I forget to ~
Breathe.
This simple act of life has almost left me now.
The joy that I felt has been replaced with pain beyond my understanding.
I wish for peace; I wish for my simple life to return
And for the love and pleasures that I have known to accompany me
again.
Dare I take a moment now and tear myself away from this anguish.
I do.
And in your Light, I find the strength to let go.
To trust,
to believe
that all will be well,
all will be blessed
and all will be in Divine Order.
My breath returns and I sense lightness within my heart.
Tears run down my face, yet these are not tears of sadness; they are tears
of joy,

a feeling that I have not felt for a very long time.

Thank you gentle Spirit
for holding me,
for loving me
and for allowing me once again to sense your presence.
I know ~ I must remember this.
I must remember to allow your light to guide me, to give me strength.
For I too often wrap myself up with the burdens of life,
giving away my power,
and making life my own struggle, in my own right.
I forget that life does not have to be this way, for you are always near.
So I remember now ~ how important my connection is to you
and how I did not come to this earth alone,
but with the Spiritual strength and the blessings of thousands who watch
over me
and who protect me every moment.

Chapter Four

Somehow, Holly was back at work within 30 days of having a torso-length tumor sliced out of her.

But what started out as a nearly normal day at work for her was shredded instantly by a call from the health center doctor who had performed her surgery. The doctor coldly explained that the biopsy revealed many cancer cells mixed in with the other cells of the tumor, and since the cyst had been drained, there was a chance that some of the cancer cells had entered her body and attached themselves to any or all of her major organs. The doctor wanted Holly to go back into the hospital immediately and have biopsies performed on all of her major organs. He said that if this procedure wasn't done right away, she could die.

Holly called me from work hysterical. I was very upset about the fact that they wanted to open her up again for this kind of procedure *and* I was enraged that a professional physician had the nerve to deliver this kind of information to my daughter at *work*. How dare they call someone at work informing them that they could die? Holly told the doctor that she had to think about what she had been told. Within a few days, the doctor sent a letter to our home for Holly to sign, saying that he was not responsible for anything that happened to her if she did not listen to his advice.

It certainly would be a wonderful thing if people could always share the true love in their hearts. I wonder if this doctor would have handled things the same way if he were delivering this message, which he gave Holly, to a member of his own family.

I am sure that the doctor sent the letter to protect himself from people who insist on turning our society upside-down by suing for every little thing. Is all the coldness we project based on our love for money—or our fear of losing it?

> *I reflect on the saying in the Bible "Do unto others as you would have them do unto you." I wonder if its true meaning is that we should always love, for what love we give, we get. But if we hate or do wrong to others, does this not come back to us too? I try and remember that my thoughts and actions, good and bad, go out and come back. This gives the Do Unto Others saying a powerful new energy of its own.*

When Holly came home from work that day, looking more drained than she did post-operatively, we all sat down and talked about what had happened. Holly said that she really didn't want to go back into the hospital again. I told her that it would be all right, even though deep inside, I was scared to death for her and wished desperately that there were something I could do to relieve the fear that she was going through. I told her that we would go to another doctor and get a second opinion.

We called the hospital and picked up the biopsy results. We needed to have the exact wording of what the medical team had found. I then started talking to people and asking them if they knew anything about this form of cancer. No one really knew what it was. I again went to the library and found that there had been only *seven* cases of this type of cancer reported *in the United States*—no wonder no one had heard of it before. The book also said that this particular cancer had a tendency to attach itself to any of the patient's major organs. Thank God some of the books listed a few doctors that had worked with patients who had gone through this, and I immediately tried to contact them for their advice. Although we prayed for some quick answers to our questions, no one got back to us right away.

Days turned into weeks; every time we needed a lab report, Holly had to go to the hospital to sign it out and sign it back in. This was done about five times, and each doctor we approached did not really know what to tell us. One doctor to whom I had written about Holly's situation contacted me from Virginia. He was nice enough to tell us that there really wasn't much he could do at that distance, but he would be willing to look at my daughter's records if we wanted to mail them down to him. We decided not to send her records because of the distance. By this point I had made an appointment for Holly at Sloan Kettering Hospital in New York City. The weeks had now turned into months and we were all concerned that the cancer could already be spreading to the major organs of Holly's body without us even knowing how or where it had spread.

I found myself wondering how my mom had been able to hold herself together when *she* found out that my dad had cancer in 1966. My parents were in their 40's then. I guess working three jobs back then had helped keep mom's mind pretty occupied. Like her, I now found that when a loved one needs you, a person does whatever she can for that loved one, even if some days, you think it might kill you.

In 1966, my dad was out of work; the newspapers were merging again. He had built a darkroom in the basement so he could take on some jobs to help my mom out while he was sick. He was much too kind and not much of a businessman: most of his work he basically gave away. Our family expenses were going through the roof; the expensive medications that my dad had to take for his sickness cost a small fortune. My mom did all that she could to make ends meet by working during the day as a bookkeeper for a builder named Mario Bummara, at night at Macys, and on weekends at a local garage, also as a bookkeeper. She would come home from work beyond exhausted and would often have a drink to help her relax. She never let my brother or me know how she felt and she ended up many a night, I later learned, in the basement crying and praying that things would be all right.

My brother and I spent a lot of time with our friends during this period; it was a way to escape the unspoken sadness in our home. I also turned to Joe for comfort, and we would spend hours on the phone talking at night, without my parents knowing. We would wait until they were asleep and then I would sneak downstairs at the designated time and make the phone call. I wrapped myself up in whatever love he was willing to give me. I felt that, somehow, what he felt about me was who I really was. I never recognized that I was a long way from knowing my true self, my strength, and my independence.

~

Over time, I made a good friend at the library where I was working. Alba was an older woman, and I looked up to her. She was like a second mom to me and would listen to all of the problems that I was going though. She felt that my mom was over-protective. In a non-insulting way, she taught me that mom should let me try to do more on my own, and stop worrying so much about me.

Alba couldn't believe that when I was 19 years-old, my mom would bring my dinner to work every night; I knew that mother's reason was so she could be certain that I would eat right.

It wasn't until I had my own children that I began to understand some of what mother must have felt: how she was trying to save the world that we lived in at that time; how she wanted her family to be safe, healthy, and taken care of. Her love for us was so strong, stronger than I could ever imagine love could be. She would have given her life for us if she had to, if it would have made things right. Thank God she was a strong person, because our family at that time needed someone to protect us, someone we could count on, and someone who would guide us through those troubled times. She was teaching me how to be strong then, even though I did not know it. In those trying times, she was my example of strength, faith, and love.

~

I wanted to take every avenue I could think of to help *my* daughter. Of course the question of our family's medical history came up with each doctor that we saw. The same answer was always given: we really didn't know because I was adopted. Although this question had never bothered me much before, it was now critical that I had some answers for the sake of my daughter's health, probably even for the sake of her life. I told Holly that I would approach her grandmother and ask her for her help.

In the past when I would question my mother about my background, she would not want to talk about it. I was happy with my adopted parents, and became content with not knowing my background. Besides, part of me was afraid of what truths I might find, cause sometimes the truth hurts.

The dreams and hopes of our lives are important to us. God has given us the opportunity to create what we need. I have found it important when you pray, to be very specific about what you ask for, for you usually get exactly what you request. We need to be prepared to accept what we might find when we stray from our true life's path. God tries to guide us, but we still can choose the direction we want to go.

At 20 years old, I needed to acquire a passport to move to Germany where my first husband was going to be stationed. I filled out the application and sent in all of the important paperwork including my birth certificate. A few weeks went by and I got a response from Albany saying that the date on the seal of my birth certificate was not within the legal time limit of my birth date. The correspondence from the state's capital added that there were three reasons for this, one of which was adoption. They needed me to bring in my adoption papers to the passport office in New York City. I was concerned about asking my mom for the paperwork; I knew how she felt about me bringing up my adoption. Thank goodness she had at least told me of my adoption prior to this, for I would have been enraged and distraught if this was the way I found out.

Reluctantly she took me into New York, never showing me the adoption paperwork. When we arrived, we stood on line for quite a long time until it was finally our turn and my mom handed the paperwork to the man behind the counter. He looked at the papers then looked at me and asked if I was Ka... J.. Sky. I could not understand what he said cause when he began to say the name my mom almost jumped over the counter to kill him. She obviously did not want me to hear or know my real name that was evidently on the papers. The man then meekly took the information he needed and gave my mom back the paperwork, which she quickly put in her purse. She was obviously concerned that I would take the information and look for my real family. I feel that she was afraid that she would lose me and was held hostage by the enduring insecurity and fear that another family would one day win my love. During my life I had tried to show my mother that I loved her and wanted her to know that even though we didn't always get along, my love for her would always be there; yet, for some reason I never felt that I'd be able to truly assure her of this.

Many years after that trip into New York City was burned into my memory, I faced my daughter's cancer, and I knew next to nothing about my family history. I set a lunch date with my mom; my intent was to bring up the subject of the adoption paperwork.

I was very nervous as the day approached and was worried that my mother would not help me. I tried to think positively, but my past experiences on the subject had taken me nowhere.

Finally, I was sitting in front of my mother having lunch, petrified to pop the question, yet at the same time knowing that my daughter's health was on the line. I explained that the doctors wanted to know about our family history since they had found this rare form of cancer in Holly. I asked her if there might be any information on the adoption papers that would be helpful, knowing full well that I remembered the incident in New York where the man almost said my birth name. My mom could not understand why family history was important and I tried to explain it to her. Finally, she looked at me and said she didn't know anything that could help us. I knew that she was lying, but was in total shock that she would deny her granddaughter helpful information, knowing how serious Holly's condition was. I was beyond angry, and I didn't know what else to say. I loved my mother and respected her and did not want to hurt her, but for my daughter, what was I going to do? When Holly heard what had happened, she too was very upset even though I told her why her grandmother was probably afraid to give us the information.

A week or two went by and the fact that my mom would not help me was digging deeper and deeper into me. I knew that I had to ask my mom again. I thought to myself that I had to be firmer and tell her that I needed the adoption papers so that I could at least make an attempt to look for *some* family history.

I had to remind myself how powerful our minds are. I needed to remember that God is always there, ready to listen to us. I needed to release the negativity and fear that I was holding inside of me. I had experienced this wonderful power of manifestation one evening when I was getting ready to go to a holiday dinner party held by my husband's boss. I had attended that event the previous few years and had consistently had a terrible time. I hated going and being the token wife and listening to the men talk about work. I never knew what to say to the other women and usually couldn't wait for the evening to end. Here I was getting ready and sarcastically thinking it was going to be another great night out. I had read about positive thinking but had really never tried to make it work for me. As I was standing in the mirror putting on my makeup, I thought that I certainly wasn't doing myself any good by thinking it was going to be another crappy night. Right then and there I started to change my thoughts. I imagined that this time the evening was going to be different. I was going to walk in and meet new people with whom I would have no trouble talking and would have a wonderful time. I imagined the whole evening in my mind in as much detail as possible with every positive aspect that I could think of. As it turned out, the evening was just as I had hoped. I had truly manifested a wonderful night for myself. We often do not realize how much we can get out of positive thinking and communication with God

I was afraid to confront my mom again, but remembered that if I really wanted her to assist Holly and me with the information that we needed, I had to *imagine* my mother actually giving me the adoption papers and helping me. I did this for a few days before I set up another lunch date with her in order to ask her for her help again. This time was different. I told mom that we could at least learn about Holly's nationality and background from my birth name that I knew was on the adoption papers. I asked her if maybe she could at least give me the paperwork, since I knew that that information was on it. I was amazed when this time she said yes, she would not only give me the name but also the paperwork, even though— she felt compelled to add—none of this would probably do me any good. I had the paperwork within a few days.

There it was on the top, my birth name: Kathy Jane Segur

Kathy Jane Segur. My very first name on earth.

I read through the rest of the information quickly. Mother was right; there wasn't much else on this paper to help Holly. Where was I going to start? What was I going to do? I needed this information as soon as possible. My mind raced with different ideas; the search was on.

Within the span of just a few days, I called adoption agencies, adoption departments, the Capitol in Albany, International Soundex Reunion Registry, State of New York Heath Department, and the Office of Vital Records in Rochester, New York, the town where I was born; I wrote 160 letters to other agencies for their help, another 60 letters to my legislators, and from most received no reply at all. The bottom line was that my files were closed, and it would take a *court order* to open them. I was told that I could hire a lawyer, but *unless someone was dying* it was very unlikely any files would be opened or information of any kind given. The truth was: my daughter *could* be dying. But I didn't have the time or money necessary to wage the sadly required bureaucratic and legal warfare.

I could not believe how much trouble I was having. How cruel were the laws of the state: that when someone really needed help and could die, the state would continue to 'protect' people of prior generations and not give the *current* generation—the adopted child and her own ailing progeny—vital, potentially life-saving information of the most personal nature? Why was an anonymous group of people in the state capital privy to the most intimate parts of my own identity—including clues to my family's health history, while *I* was not? I was at a loss and did not know what else to do but to pray, pray, pray. I prayed.

Connection

Transforming our lives
into the beautiful people that we came here to become
can be a process.
Efforts of Divine Energy are sent through us,
yet the world and its constant struggles keep
these messages away form our conscious minds.

We do not take the time to connect,
not only with the Divine
but with our fellow man,
for we assume too much
and believe that we know and have knowledge of how others feel.

We block ourselves form the unification that God asks of us.
Each one born into this life having a special gift, a gift or treasure
not to be hidden
but to be shared with others
and brought into wholeness and unified form.

We were not born to be alone.
We were meant to share with others
and within this process
to glorify God's Name

God: who lives through each of us and as each of us.

Live each day as if it were your last;
don't wait to give yourself to the universal energy
The All That Is
that waits for us to express itself through us.
Live in the moment
and allow Spirit to come through you
and enhance your life and your daily activities.
Connect to others with a greater understanding,
an open mind, and acceptance.
Your acceptance will not only fortify your being,
but others' being-ness, and the world's.

Chapter Five

Prayer took me a long way, but my anxiety intensified. As we pursued various new doctors in an effort to dissolve Holly's problem, Holly, Bill, my husband, and I did what we could to keep our spirits up, always trying to maintain a positive attitude; I did not want to upset Holly with the horrors that filled my imagination and that might lie ahead for her. Bill, Holly's husband, didn't want to talk about things at all. I guess he kept hoping that Holly was fine and that everything would just go away.

Of course everyone else hoped that Holly was healthy too, but after the doctor told Holly that she could die if the problem were ignored, no one could take the chance and just be idle.

This whole experience was life-altering for Holly, physically and spiritually.

It was for me too:

I escaped into my own little world, whenever I could, by roller-blading at the park to music, praying for hours and releasing my sorrows through my tears.

During my life, I have had many conversations with people about mediation. A recurring theme has been how much these friends and other people would like to meditate, but how difficult they find it to do. Others have thought that in order to achieve good results in meditation, one must let one's mind go totally blank. I tell these people that I too used to believe that this was the only way to meditate, but I also add this: why can't true meditation come in many forms?

If one removes herself from her everyday environment and takes a step toward putting her mind in a different place, isn't that meditating? I told a friend of mine once that he could actually meditate when he went <u>skiing</u>. I asked him to try to forget about his everyday problems and to remain mentally in the moment—focused entirely on what he was doing. I suggested that he enjoy nature and his surroundings and try to let God speak to him each time he climbed the hill to make his next run. He was not required to perform any special ritual: he did not need to light a candle, put himself in a quiet room, cross his legs, or let his mind go blank. He tried the simple idea that I suggested, and— even during his first experience—was amazed at the powerful way in which this conscious focus worked for him. It was a surprise for him, for he never thought about meditating in this manner.

Every day, all of us take time to meditate, even if we do not realize it: whether we are standing in line, waiting at a traffic light, or daydreaming: our spirits face these countless opportunities to arrive in a state of heightened awareness. It is our conscious participation that transforms these wonderful gifts of time into peace- and awareness-building meditation.   We just need to live more in the moment and take the time to ask God to fill our hearts with His presence and with peace...or recognize that He is doing so always.

It was moments like these—as I was roller-blading and praying for my daughter—that I found some time for peace.

With my continuous and persistent activity of arranging doctor appointments for Holly, asking experts for advice on her condition, and letting family members know how Holly was feeling, I was spending many hours each day on the telephone. One evening Bill came in from work, overhearing me on the phone *again,* speaking about his wife—my daughter. When I hung the phone up, he started *yelling* at me, asking me why I had to tell the *world* about Holly and *their* business. Not wanting to make a scene in front of the other household members, I asked him to step outside so that I could speak to him in private.

I was angry, completely exhausted, and terribly upset. Bill had no idea where I was coming from. With tears in my eyes, I told him that he had no right to tell me what to do. In no uncertain terms I said, "This is my daughter, and I will talk to a million people if I have to, to try and get her the help that she needs. I will not stop until she is better. I lost my dad to cancer and I am not about to lose Holly."

Bill became completely quiet; he had never seen me this upset before. Holly and Bill had been married for a little over two years at this point. They had lived far away from me. Bill hardly knew me—and he had no clue about our family's history. I began to tell him the following story:

My dad faced cancer—and was ravaged by it. He went through many years of hell from being sick with it. He had tremendous trouble eating, and the doctors had tried stretching his esophagus, hoping that if there were any blockages, stretching this long tube inside him would remove them. Dad was better for a while, but within a few months, the doctors were talking about doing major surgery. They put my father into the hospital for a second time, and he went through a five-hour operation, where they found cancer in his esophagus and stomach. During that operation, they had to remove half of his stomach and half of his esophagus. He was over 6 feet tall, had been a heavy man, and was down to 105 pounds.

The operation was devastating for my father and the whole family. Dad had 99 stitches across his back. Being the relentlessly jovial man that he was, Dad joked that they should have made it an even 100. I always admired my father's courage. He was an amazing person, always keeping a smile on his face, so no one would know what kind of pain he was going through.

Both of my parents tried to keep as much of what was happening with my dad between them, trying to protect my brother and me, even though we were in our late teens. I wish they could have shared more of their love and concern with us. I wanted so much to share mine and to help them in some way, but our family was known for not sharing their feelings. All of our emotions were kept under the covers, and the love that I wanted to extend and receive was lost, even when it was needed most.

However, through the pain, we were blessed one day with one thing in our house that both gave and received unconditional love: our dog, Snoopy.

I had always wanted an animal that I could enjoy, but my mom would say: "If it's not in a cage, you can't have it." So we were blessed with birds, mice, and gerbils. All wonderful pets—but none sharing the potential for fun, love, and bonding as much as a dog.

One year when my brother was very sick from school, his first-grade class was in the process of hatching chicken eggs. Once he recovered and went back to school, he saw that all the other children's eggs had hatched and the children had taken home their own cute little yellow baby chicks. There was one egg left waiting for my brother that still hadn't hatched. A chick finally made his way into the world one day, but he was as black as the ace of spades. He was a male, not a cute yellow chick, but a *rooster*. My brother was so proud. He didn't care if his chick was unusual, and I bet in a way, he was happy his chick was different compared to the others. From the day he brought the rooster home, there was constant noise. My mom wasn't happy about the noise or the steady work of taking care of him. She finally convinced my brother to give him a new home at a place called Zorn's, a locale where I am sure he lived the rest of his life being very reproductive and perhaps even fulfilled.

One day, out of the blue, my mom asked my brother and me if we would like to go and pick out a *bunny*. I was flabbergasted and shocked!

I wondered if Mom had lost her mind or had become exceptionally compassionate because my dad was sick and she knew that he loved animals. I didn't care. It wasn't exactly what my brother and I had in mind for a pet, but I certainly was not going to look a gift horse in the mouth. So off we went to the store to look at bunnies. Once there, we picked out an adorable bunny rabbit with big ears, but my mom was shocked when the shop owner explained to her what kind of work was involved in taking care of rabbits. My mom knew that my brother and I always wanted a dog, so she turned to us and said, "How would you guys like to go pick out a puppy?" We couldn't believe our ears, we were so happy. This was what we had always wanted. That day, we brought home the cutest little mutt and named her Snoopy.

I never felt such unconditional love.

Snoopy filled a void that had long been in my heart. I would hold her in my arms at night. Her fur pressed up against my nose, I would listen to her breath. It was so soothing. Even when my dad was sick, Snoopy was there to comfort him. She would sit by his side and keep him company, when no one else was at home. I always enjoyed watching the two of them together, knowing that Snoopy was always there for him with her never-ending love. She was an angel in disguise and a blessing to our family when we so very much needed her.

I reflect back at this time in my life with greater understanding today of why this dog meant so much to me then. It was a few years ago, as I was doing a past life regression with a lady named Elizabeth, that I came to a new understanding about myself: During this regression I saw myself as a struggling artist in France, lying on the balcony of my apartment building. My head was resting on a large black French poodle, and I felt so much love and peace as I looked up at the stars. For some reason, this simple pleasure was so important to me. Elizabeth asked me to see if I knew what year it was. The year 1789 popped into my head. At the time of the regression, this didn't mean that much to me. Historical dates and times were not my forte, in my current life, since I had failed social studies. After the regression, I questioned what I had seen in my mind, until I came home and put the year into the computer to see what would come up. Lo-and-behold it turned out that it was the year of the French Revolution. This was clearly an extremely challenging and stress-filled time in a past life associated with my being. It was then that this dog gave me a special moment of love and peace, as my head lay on its belly. Discovering this new history of myself, I understood both intuitively and metaphysically, why in this life, I find animals so exceptionally endearing.

My father grew sicker and sicker. I would watch him at night lying on his bed, his stomach sunken in as he tried to find the strength to heave up any blood or food that would get caught in his throat. I could hardly bear looking at him and watching him suffer. "He is a good man," I said to God, "why are you doing this to him?!"

My dad finally ended up in the hospital again and was there for a long time. My mom wanted to keep us from seeing him with tubes down his throat and other hospital hook-ups. Of course, she did not tell us of her reasons. All I knew was that we were 16 and 19 years old and it had been months since I had seen my dad. I am sure she also wanted to keep from us the fact that he was dying, but I wasn't stupid; I knew how sick he was and how much suffering and pain he had been through. I began to pray nightly that God would either heal him or take him in His arms to heaven.

One day my mom and my brother picked me up from the library where I was working. My mom asked us on the way home if we would like to go to the hospital to see my dad. Of course we both said yes. I will never forget that night. I was able to hold Dad's hand through the oxygen tent and tell him that I loved him. After a while, my mom wanted me to leave so that she could have a little time alone with my dad. I left reluctantly, for something inside told me that I might not see him again. He died early the next morning at 45 years young, during my last year of high school. He was respected and loved by all who had met him, with his constant smile and wonderful sense of humor that stayed with him to the very end.

Wakes, funerals and burials are difficult times for most families and this was no different for ours. My mom tried to stay strong for both my brother and me. She refused to cry in front of us. We never knew about the nights she spent, after we were in bed, locked in the darkroom in the basement, where she would pound the walls from the pain and sorrow that she felt. It was actually during one of my mom's and my many arguments that I learned about her feelings. She was telling me that she had gone through more than I would ever realize with my father's death. She said I would never know how she felt and how many times she would go down into the basement and cry alone to protect my brother and me from the sadness and torment that she was going through. How could I have known any of this? I wanted to be part of her life, but she kept this to herself only to release the guilt upon me at the most unexpected and inopportune times.

My brother always had put my dad on a pedestal. Dad meant everything to him; my father was the perfect man in my brother's eyes. I don't think my brother really knew how ill my dad was, and I know he did not expect him to die. He held onto my mother after my dad was buried and cried in her arms as they sat on her bed. I can remember that night as if it were yesterday, and my heart went out to both of them. I prayed that there was something that I could do or say, but I was at a loss.

Of course, I was sad too. However I did not want to see my dad suffer anymore; besides, my prayer had been answered, and God had taken Dad home to paradise. I was close to my dad, and I knew I would miss his love and beautiful energy, but I was glad that God had eased his pain, and I knew in my heart that he was finally at peace.

I feel that our family could have used some counseling after my father's death, for we never did really express our feelings to each other. That was the Higgins way. We just picked ourselves up and went on. I saw the sadness in my mom's and my brother's eyes, and I wanted to share my feelings too but it never was to be. Even today, more than 30 years later, I sense a sadness in my brother's heart. I really believe that my father's death had more of an impact on Gordon than he may ever admit. Even now, as I write this book, we are not very close, for our paths have gone two different ways. I love my brother with all my heart and have wondered what might happen if we ever took the time to go back to that moment and just express our love for each other and what we had to go through. I have imagined in my mind the two of us doing this; holding each other and letting go of the pain that we both have held inside for all these years.

We often hate it when a loved one is taken from us. We try to make sense of it all. We usually get mad at God for not allowing our beloved to fulfill his or her life. Who is to say that our beloved didn't though? Maybe we choose before we get here how long we will live. God and our souls only are the ones that know this truth. We are not just here for ourselves to grow, but also to make our mark on the world and to help others to learn.

This might explain why children die. What lessons are we learning as they leave us behind? What growth is ours to obtain? Could there be a universal purpose that only the child's death fulfilled, whereby those that were left behind were inspired to take action that they otherwise may not have? Maybe we make a sacred contract with God before we come here? Death should not be something we fear. It is only a transition from one place to the next; for our soul never dies.

Snoopy continued to keep us company for a while after my dad's death and even my mom, who wasn't too thrilled about getting a dog in the first place, became attached to Snoopy's cute little ways.

No one was quite prepared for what happened one day while my brother and I were at school:

My mom had let Snoopy out to run to the park that was only two doors away, when the children across the street innocently called her name. As destiny would have it, Snoopy responded to their calls, and while running to greet them, she was hit by a passing car and killed. My mom had no idea how she was going to tell us. We had recently lost our dad, but now to lose our dog. The pain in her heart was unbearable. Somehow, she found the strength. Hearing the news made me sick to my stomach. I cried for days. To this day, I have wonderful memories of my dad and Snoopy and feel fortunate to have had them both in my life, even if it was for a short while. They gave me hope, strength, love, and many blessings. Not one precious moment is forgotten and their lives have enhanced my growth in so many ways. I have been fortunate since then to have been a part of other animals' lives, each one, in its own way, giving me love and blessing me with spiritual strength.

It is said that animals are among God's special creatures, angels in disguise. They are most in-tune with their surroundings and tend to know when we are happy or sad. They are a blessing for those of us who have them and can be the only true living source of unconditional love we ever receive in our lives.

The last year of high school, my boyfriend Joe (whom I had dated for four years) asked me to marry him. He bought me a small ring, since that was all he could afford, but I thought it was the most beautiful thing in the world. At the time, my mom and I had been struggling with our relationship. There was even more stress than previously between us since my father had died. When Joe's parents and my mom found out about our engagement, they all went berserk. They reprimanded us and told us that we were way too young to think about marriage and demanded that we break it off. I had been dating Joe since my last year in junior high school and did not want to break our engagement. I was beginning college, and Joe's parents wanted the same for him. They told us to go for a walk and seriously think over everything they had been telling us. We walked and walked, talking about how we felt. We were so much in love, but our parents with their strong influence, made us reluctantly decide to break off our engagement. Not being able to marry when we wanted to, started our relationship on a downhill slide, until it finally ended during my first year of college.

I really did love Joe, and felt I would never want any other guy.

The break with Joe sent me into a depression; it left me wondering if I would ever find anyone like him again. I hated God for all that he had done to me. Life was hell! If God was so good why would he take away my father, my dog, and turn my relationship with my boyfriend upside-down. It was the first time in my life that I felt I didn't want to live. What was the point? Life sucked and no one seemed to care if I lived or died.

In the past, art had sometimes comforted me. I had done well with art in high school and thought art would be the right move for me in college. I worked as hard as I could and would be up till all hours of the night trying to get a good grade. But now? I found it hard to believe that my teachers could be so critical of my work. I barely passed most of my projects and on the one where I had spent the least amount of time, my teacher gave me an "A." There was no rhyme or reason to their grading and anyway who were they to judge my work? Wasn't I a good artist; wasn't art all in the eye of the beholder? I got more and more depressed. Art was the one last thing I thought I could do and it too seemed to be going down the toilet.

I felt I couldn't share the problems I was going through with my mom. She had been through enough with my father's death and would come home exhausted every night from work. She was trying to pay the final hospital bills, put food on the table, and take care of my brother and me. She had enough burdens and I didn't want to upset her, besides it seemed that every time we tried to talk, we would argue. I would begin a conversation by trying to make a point, fighting back if I had to, hoping to explain my feelings, but she always seemed to know just what to say; "Don't you love me?" "Why would you do that?" "You know better!" "Did you learn that from your friend? My Chrissa [my parents' nickname for me] would never do that." It was pointless trying to communicate with her.

I prayed and prayed for happiness, but my life just seemed to get worse. I needed help, but where was I going to get it? I was mad at the world and was done being walked all over. Something inside me clicked. Instead of capitulating to life, I decided and vowed that I would never give up. I would somehow get away from all of this and make it on my own. But where was I going to go? I had no money and nowhere to live. Somehow I would make things work.

> *This of course was the problem. I was going to make it work. I wouldn't let go long enough to listen to God and let Him help me. I was bound and determined to do my thing without a thought as to what was really good or possible for me. I didn't stop for a moment to ask God if I was going off-track or if what I was doing was for my highest good. It didn't matter—God wasn't really part of my life anymore, anyway and I didn't care what he thought. I know now that if maybe I had focused on Him even for a short while, I possibly could have saved myself a lot of unnecessary pain and anguish.*

Such were the thoughts and memories swirling through my mind as Bill stood in stunned silence, contemplating my role in his wife's life.

Through all of our efforts and talking with other people, Holly, Bill, Bob, and I decided to make an appointment for Holly at Sloan Kettering Hospital in New York. It is one of the best hospitals for cancer research and we hoped that this world-class institution would give us some insight on what to do about Holly's possible condition.

The day finally arrived for us to go to Sloan Kettering and to speak to the head of oncology. We had previously submitted to Sloan Kettering all of Holly's information, but the lead doctor still wanted to examine my daughter. We met with the doctor after her exam, and he told us that Holly's case was very unusual. He had never personally experienced this particular form of cancer. Since there were so few cases of this type of cancer on record in the United States, Sloan Kettering convened a very rare meeting comprising 10 doctors specifically to discuss Holly's unusual case. Not one of them came up with a definite solution. The head of oncology told us that the results of the board's discussion were that there was really no right or wrong with Holly's situation. In his opinion, opening her up again for biopsies would *not* accomplish much. He did feel that she should be watched closely and that she should have a CAT scan done right away and, of course, that she should see her gynecologist often. He said she should continue to go for CAT scans at first every 6 months for a year or two and then once a year after that. At the end of 4 or 5 years, he felt that if there were no sign of cancer, she should be all right for the long-haul.

We were so relieved that we wanted to cry. We had been hoping and praying that Holly would not have to go through another major operation. The doctor told us what we had been praying to hear. We knew that it would be a rough road for Holly and she would have to watch herself carefully, but we were given some long needed hope.

Hope. It is amazing how much we all need it. For isn't it true that most of us can conquer the world if we have it. It gives us strength, helps us move on with our lives, and brings peace to each waking moment.

The Roads That We take

The voyage of life
The roads that we take
The passion
The fear
And all the mistakes
The hardships, the pain
The loves that we share
Which enrich all our souls
And fulfill all our cares

For life's journey is rough
For that's what life should be
The trials;
tribulations
Of all humanity
For not only do we learn
From the mistakes that we make
It helps God understand
The whole human race.

The fact we are one

With the almighty ghost
Tells us of God's love
That exceeds coast to coast
His infinite power
Reaches out to us all
As He experiences through us
The old and the small.

So we should see our burdens
Then put them aside
Enjoy every moment
Of this marvelous ride
Through recovery and joy
With the Divine from Above…
touching our hearts
With all of His love.

Chapter Six

I never thought that I would have been able to go to college, but somehow in 1970 at the age of 19, I was accepted to the New York Institute of Technology on Long Island, where I could take art courses. Art was one subject area I thought that I might be able to do well, even though I had received little or no encouragement in this field.

I was going through a depression since I had broken up with Joe, and our family had separated emotionally since my father had passed, so I figured there really wasn't much more to lose in taking a risk by attending this school that had accepted me.

My mother wanted me to go to college—I think she hoped that I would do well and fall into a career that would be something I'd enjoy. She herself had gone to trade school to become a bookkeeper, and although she did not do much with her experience during the first part of her marriage, this skill-set turned out to be a Godsend and a blessing later, when she was widowed and had to go to work to support two children. I knew my mom, and I am sure that in the back of her mind, she felt that any kind of education for me was worthwhile.

I was scared. I wasn't that fond of school to begin with. I was told that college was hard, and I was concerned about the pressure that I might be up against. I still lacked confidence in myself at this time, and I know that although part of me hoped all would be well, I was mostly frightened within. The driving force for me behind going to school was that I wanted to make my mom proud. So off to college I went.

The experience turned out to be more of a struggle than I had even expected, and there were nights that I was up till two in the morning working on a project, only to end up with a 'D'. I couldn't understand my professors' way of thinking and how these instructors did their grading. Deep inside, I felt that as long as a person was trying hard and doing something creative, the person should receive a grade higher than a 'D'. How could one person really judge another's *creative* work? Wasn't beauty in the eye of the beholder? After all, I had followed the instruction and done everything that my professors had asked. I had to almost laugh when my one project that received an 'A' came form a **Disney** movie! It certainly wasn't even *my* original idea. There seemed to be no rhyme or reason to life, and I grew more and more depressed.

> *Reflecting back on what I went through during my years in school as a child, and knowing that we as adults and parents really shouldn't coddle our children, I have to wonder if it is really so wrong to give a bit of encouragement now and then when a child is trying so hard. We, as a society, seem to be very quick to criticize but not very quick to lend a kind word of hope, faith, and belief in what others pour their hearts into.*

Even through my darkest thoughts and feelings, Jeanine was always there for me, and I looked forward to our time together. She was the one shining star in my life. She too had been going through rough times with her family, and we held on to each other emotionally for dear life. One night, Jeanine and I decided to have a "Girls Night Out" and went to the skating rink. We were both excited, and of course like most young girls, we were hoping to meet some cute guys. We did get lucky, or at least I thought so at the time, to meet two. Jeanine and I exchanged telephone numbers with them, and it wasn't long before the one that I was with, named Donald, was calling me. We began going out on dates, but as usual my mother wasn't very happy. She never seemed to like any of my friends in the past and had talked me into breaking off my engagement with Joe. This time, with everything else that was going wrong in my life, I was determined that she wasn't going to tell me whom I could or couldn't date. So, I ignored her, kept dating Donald, and even got engaged. I thought I was in love with this boy and wanted to marry him. My mom was furious and tried to change my mind. When she saw I wasn't budging, she tried to stop me from getting married by telling me she would not come to the wedding if I married him. This was her last line of hope, but it did not stop me; I planned the wedding without her, borrowed Donald's sister's dress, had Jeanine there as my maid of honor, and ran away from home without telling my mother. For three days—including the wedding day itself—I did not call my mom and tell her where I was. I had no idea at that time the pain that I had caused her. I was determined to make it on my own and didn't have a clue what a destructive path I had chosen; I only thought that I was finally going be happy.

Depression can be a devastating thing and can disrupt your entire way of thinking and life. And that is where I was when I ran away from home. I wanted to be cared for, I wanted to be loved and have someone appreciate me and who I was as a person. I felt isolated at home and I could not connect to my mom, who she was, or how she felt. I sensed love from Donald who seemed to care about me and what I was going through. I wanted to get away from my old life and start a new one that would finally be full of joy and hope. I did not know that what I was really doing was jumping out of the "pan" and into the "fire!"

At the end of the three days, I called my mom and told her what I had done and that my new husband and I were moving to Virginia. Donald had just joined the service, so I knew there wasn't much she could do or say. Unfortunately my mother's fears came true three months after Donald and I settled in Virginia.

My life was turned upside down again as Donald started beating me.

What I didn't know at the time was that my new husband suffered from manic depression, and he had survived two brain hemorrhages as a child. (His mother told me later about her son's problems, months after we were married). Life was just too much for my first husband mentally. He was drafted into the service, had to move away from home to Virginia, had the responsibility of putting food on the table, and was stuck taking care of a new wife on a Private's salary. I knew his depression was one of the reasons that he was beating me. I, of course, went into my normal 'fix-it' mode and wanted so much to help him. I wanted to make things work. I wanted us to be happy, and I certainly did not want my mother to know how much trouble I was in. I was going to make our marriage work. After all, this man was my husband, for better or for worse, and I had to prove to my mom that she was wrong about us, and we could live happily ever after.

I was not going to give up. I would do anything I could to prove to my mom that I didn't make a mistake. I didn't want to look at any other possibility. I didn't want to admit that I was wrong.

I didn't want to think that this was some kind of growing experience that I needed to go through. God was only in my mind when I was down and wanting Him to give me what I wanted. I never stopped for a moment to think that He and I (deep down in my soul) knew that this path—increasingly painful as it was becoming—was the Divinely perfect route for me. I know and believe now that I promised a long time ago, before coming to this earth, to learn and to grow from this and many other experiences. Yes, I grew and became very strong, but at this time of my life, I couldn't see anything spiritual about it.

I started a visual arts job for a small store called JM Field's (similar to Woolworth's) to try and make ends meet, and did whatever I could to keep a nice home and be a good wife. Yet the beatings continued, and I started to break out in hives from the stress. Even as I write these difficult words, a lot of this part of my life I have blocked out. The mental and physical pain was often too much to bear for my conscious mind, maybe for any conscious mind. I can remember Donald yelling at me frequently, telling me that I was worthless and stupid; he would throw things—a chair, or a book, whatever happened to be nearby—through the air and across the floor; if I was lucky, I would avoid being hit. I suffered many bruises on different parts of my body, from head-to-toe, the result of airborne objects striking me or Donald just grabbing me with force. I never really knew when my husband was going to hit me. Often, we would be having a calm conversation and all I would do was ask the wrong question or do the 'wrong' thing, and he would beat me. The first thing Donald usually did was punch me in the stomach, since he knew that I would usually drop to the ground, lose my breath, and have trouble fighting him back. He would lock me in rooms for hours with no food or drink. Sometimes I was able to quietly sneak out the window to safety. He would flip out when we were in public—shaking, punching, or slapping me in the streets.

I think that the thing that surprised me the most is that people would most of the time just walk by. If I was lucky, someone would say something or push him off of me, and he would temporarily stop. Donald's disease would cause him to be up, positive, full of life, and fun to be around one minute, and then with no notice, absolutely abusive for no rhyme or reason—to the point of even cutting me with a knife between the top of my leg and my vagina, in the middle of the night when I was sleeping. I remember that day waking up screaming and dashing for a towel to stop the blood. Luckily the cut was not too deep, but to this day I still have the scar, which reminds me of that terrible time.

When I was at my wits' end, I would run away and find a place of refuge. This would allow me private time to cry and to think. I spent evenings sleeping in the balcony of the church, hiding where no one could see me. I slept in an old abandoned cabana and even outside in the rain. When I would do this, I would think *I will never go back*, but I was afraid and alone with no money and no one to turn to. I did not think my life could get any worse, and then things came to a boiling point when my eyes rolled up into my head and would not come down from the stress I was under. I tried to bring them down, but couldn't, and I begged my husband to take me to the hospital. Instead of helping, he got angry and made the already tense situation worse when he told me that I was doing it on purpose. He threatened me with a knife if I didn't stop my shit and I began to panic.

Somehow I talked Donald into taking me to the emergency room, where the doctors gave me tranquilizers. They told me to go home, take one, and wait a while to see if it would work. If it didn't, they said, I could take another one. After waiting some time and taking *both* tranquilizers, it was obvious that I was more strung out than I thought, and we were back to the emergency room again. There, the doctors gave me a shot to relax my nerves. I was finally able to settle down when I got home and got the long-needed rest I hadn't had in weeks. Even after all of that and the obvious stress that I was under, I continued to stay with Donald.

There were more surprises in store for the two of us when we heard that Donald was being sent to Germany. Although I was going to be leaving a job that I liked and leaving my few friends, I went with him, of course. We had to live *on the economy* (an army service term meaning out with the general public with no support from the army or a place to live on the base). You had to be a sergeant to be taken care of by the service. (I think the reason this was an army regulation was because the U.S. military hoped to discourage marriages of young men who were merely Privates in the service.) Our living arrangements were poor. The place was on the top floor of a home, and we had one room and a bathroom. The main room contained a bed, couch, table, armoire, and small refrigerator. The bathroom had no tub or shower, only a sink, toilet, cabinet for food and a hot plate to heat something up. Although it certainly was substandard living conditions, I did what I could to make our little apartment nice and even went back to work.

Although my husband tried to keep it from me, I found out a few months later that he was told by the army to seek private counseling. The army obviously had seen that he had some emotional problems. I asked him why he hadn't told me, and we started to argue. It was apparent that the reason he was silent was because he did not want to give me a reason to leave him. Even with the involvement of the Army, the beatings of me continued, and Donald continued to have no qualms about lashing into me in public. He hit me in front of his parents who also had nothing to say. What was wrong with this world I was living in, I thought? My life was a total nightmare.

I tried to fight back, but not only was I unable to predict *when* Donald was going to hit me, Donald was not stupid. One day, we were having a pleasant enough conversation, when I asked him if he could take out the garbage that had stacked up the last week or two. He flipped out on me and stood up and immediately punched me in the stomach, his normal tactics. This particular beating caused me to have a miscarriage.

I didn't even know I was pregnant. Thank goodness I never had a child with Donald.

> *I wanted God to fix everything. Make it all go away. Why had God deserted me and left me to deal with this pain. It never entered my mind that it was me— not He—who chose this path of destruction, and it was only me who could get me out of it. All I had to do was change my direction, but at the time I could see no other direction. I felt alone and afraid.*

I would speak to my mom now and then, but told her nothing of my situation; I certainly did not want to hear her say "I told you so, why didn't you listen to me?"

I had no money to go home, so I felt—in every cell of my body—that I couldn't leave Donald even if I wanted to.

After a year in Germany, my husband was finally granted a leave of absence, and we decided to come home and see our families. I can still remember my friend Cindy, who was the only one I confided in. She had driven us to the Stuttgart Airport in Germany, and as we were saying our good-byes, I said I would see her again soon. Somehow she intuitively knew more than me and said "No you won't; we will not see each other again." She was right.

We arrived back in the States and ended up staying at Donald's parents' house. I fell into a deep depression. I knew this was my chance to leave Donald if I was going to. I was afraid to tell my mom, couldn't afford to live on my own, and had left everything I owned behind in Germany.

Out of sheer desperation, I finally got up the nerve to tell my mom what I was going through. She had had no idea and was sick when she heard what he was doing to me. She spoke to me calmly, and told me that I had to decide what was best for me. She said that marriage was a serious matter and whatever I decided to do, to remember it was for keeps for there was no turning back. This was the first time that I understood tough love and respected my mom for her power and strength. Even after everything I had told her, she found the courage to allow me to make up my own mind. She reluctantly dropped me back home at Donald's house where we were staying, to make my decision. As I closed the door to step out of the car, she looked at me and told me that she loved me with all her heart and that she was there for me if I needed her.

> *I think this was the first time in my life that I really understood my mom and the strong, loving, powerful woman she was. I always wanted us to*

be close. Had I been as much to blame for our disconnection as she was? I cringed to think of how much I must have put her through, and yet she was still there for me, no matter what I had done. This was true love, mothers' love, the love that I would understand when I eventually had my own child.

For days I did not eat, sleep, or come out of Donald's bedroom. It had finally dawned on me what I had done, and the mess I had gotten myself into. I knew a marriage should last forever and did not like the thought of being divorced. I wanted to help Donald, but I was becoming so weak; I wanted to die, to kill myself and end it all.

No one in Donald's family even asked me how I was. On the third day self-imprisoned in Donald's bedroom, insight came to me. I promise you when I say this: that it was heaven-sent, for I was ready to do myself in when the thought came to me, and I asked myself, "If Donald is beating me what would he do to our children?" Thank goodness we did not have any children, and looking back now at the beatings that caused my miscarriage, I am blessed to not have any attachments to him. I would not have been able to make a clean break, if we would have had children together. So, mustering up the little strength I had left, I packed a few things and told Donald that I was going to go and stay with my mom for a while. Donald's family was at church when I left, for I am sure they would not have let me go. My mom, thank the Lord, opened her heart to me and let me stay with her.

I thought that I was finally free of Donald, but when he discovered that I was gone for good, he and his parents harassed me and my mom at her home. Donald tied yellow ribbons on the tree in mom's front yard in hopes that I would know of his love and come back to him. His father showed up at the house one night and told my mother that he would kill the dog that had belonged to Donald and me (the dog which I had loved and left behind), if I did not come back to his son. Donald showed up at the house one day when my mom and I were getting ready to leave. We saw him waiting outside, and as we clandestinely entered the car in the enclosed garage, my mom told me to get in and hide down on the floor in the back, where Donald couldn't see me. My mom had backed the car into the garage, so she was able to pull straight out as the door opened. As the car was exiting, Donald jumped in front of it, begging for my mom to let him talk to me. Somehow my mom found the strength to keep moving the car forward inch-by-inch without running him over—avoiding a murderous outcome, an outcome which at this point probably held a certain understandable appeal in her mind. A week didn't go by that there wasn't something occurring that didn't involve Donald or his family.

In the meantime, I was able to get a job at a company one mile from where my mom lived. For the first few months, while saving up the money to buy my mom's car, I walked back and forth to work. Things had settled down a little with Donald and his family, and just when I thought I had heard the last from him, the following happened:

I was walking home from work as usual and was passing a nearby woodsy area. Donald was lurking in the trees. He stealthily eased out of the woods without me knowing and snuck up behind me abruptly. I was shocked and terrified when I saw him. He begged me and begged me to come back to him. I walked as fast as I could, trying to get home and kept telling him No and to leave me alone. He wouldn't back down. Before I realized it, he had grabbed me and pulled me to his car that he had hidden on the side road.

The trunk was open. In what seemed like slow motion, he began the process of pushing me inside—or at least it seemed clear that's what he intended.

I was screaming for help and to leave me alone. One of the neighbors came out of her house and turned around and went back in. To this day, I don't know if she even tried to call the police or do anything, I was just blessed that my mom realized that I was a little late coming home, and had ventured out in her car to see where I was. When Donald saw her drive by, he let me go and I jumped into her car to get away.

Although my mom did her best to help me, and I truly was very grateful that she took me into her home, we still weren't getting along very well. I wanted out of her house as fast as possible, for I knew she too wanted that for me. In a way, working so hard at my job was actually a blessing, for it gave me a little less time to think, think, think.

The road to recovery wasn't an easy one, but somehow I made it through, and in three months, with my mom's help, I had worked hard enough to buy her car, pay for my own divorce, and sublet an apartment in the town of Huntington.

Sometimes in life, there are so many little things happening that we don't see the big picture. This was one of those periods for me. Then, rather suddenly, with one Divine thought, my perspective changed. The realization of my whole situation hit me in the face:

Experiencing the accumulation of years of abuse, I had brought myself currently into a depression worse than *any* I had ever experienced before. This was exceptionally terrifying, as I had experienced *many* depressions.

I wondered where I was going to get the strength to pull myself out of it. I sunk deeper and deeper into the dumps and began not to care if I lived or died. Why wasn't I more thankful about being out of the horrible situation I had escaped? I was working now from morning to night to save for a new place to live. I tackled anything the company gave me on my job, and, despite my inner state, they were pleased to have such a conscientious worker. I moved from one place to the next on the assembly line and (merely for being me?) ended up with an increase in salary working in one of the offices as a secretary.

I had made it through hell and back, I thought, but felt little confidence within myself. How could I? It was obvious that I had screwed my life up royally. What a dumb girl I was. My mind was my worst enemy. I had constant negative thoughts about myself. I was a used woman now, who would want me? I had hoped that someone would find me attractive, but would they stay with me once they found out I was divorced? Would they think what happened to me was my fault? Would they think that I seemed like a nice girl, but maybe there was something wrong with me that they couldn't see? Would they give me a chance? I was so lonely even though I was around many wonderful people. Doubts and feelings of self-loathing kept racing through my mind. Looking back, I can see that I never gave myself any credit for all of the hard work I did; I also never gave myself a chance to become whole again. All I looked at were my bad points. I had forgotten that I, too, was a child of

*God, a loving caring person, trying to find her way
in this confusing world.*

My dear friend Jeanine was very supportive, but I longed
for a man to love. No one seemed interested in me, and I
decided to call Joe (my old boyfriend) to see how he was
doing. I prayed that us getting back together would do
the trick, make me feel whole again and loved. As I
picked up the phone, I wondered if he was dating anyone
else—or worse—married. Thank goodness he wasn't, and
we started dating again. So much had changed since the
last time we were together. He had a band now that was
working full-time and he had single-handedly
constructed a sound studio in his basement. I was so
happy to be with him again, but I had grown up too fast,
and we were both very different now. I tried to get back
that feeling of young love and the connection that we had
shared for more than four years, but it just wasn't there.
I didn't want to entertain doubts, I just wanted to be
with him; I was just so lonely. He had been my first love,
and I was hoping with all of my soul that, with enough
time, the old feelings I had in my heart would come back
again. With this hope inside me, we stayed together.

*The human race tends to reach out and extend their
hands and support to those in need. Most of us do
this quickly with love and compassion when
someone needs help. This human caring gift was
visibly given when the Twin Towers fell in NY and
again when the great tsunami of Christmas 2004
hit Sri Lanka and many other countries. Those from
near and far came to assist those people in need.
But what happens when we personally need
something? Do we stop to give ourselves the
strength, love, and nurturing caring that our bodies
and minds so desperately need? I did not know*

how to do this for myself when I was going through my divorce. I wanted to feel love, and needed help, but looked for it to be given to me by <u>others</u>, for I did not know how to give it to myself.

One of the electronic engineers who worked at my job would come by frequently, pretending to see how things were going on the assembly line where I was working; I was oblivious to his flirting. I thought he was being nice. After all, I was going out with Joe again, and meeting someone else was barely a thought in my consciousness. The engineer's name was Bob, and he dressed so funny in his Mickey Mouse shirt, baggy green corduroys, and construction boots. He certainly wasn't one of the best-dressed men I had ever seen. We got talking one day, and he asked me if I had ever been horseback riding. I told him 'once or twice,' but I wasn't very good at it. He told me about this nice place that he had gone to for horseback riding and then asked me if I wanted to go riding with him. I accepted. I hadn't gone out with anyone else since my divorce and really not that many other men in my whole life. Things between Joe and me weren't that great, and I am sure this was the dominant reason why I said yes to the date with Bob.

We had a good time; he was very funny, and we had a lot to talk about. I didn't know if he would ask me out again, and it really didn't matter, but a few weeks later he did. This time it was to a big affair at the Colony Hill, a fancy catering hall. I was very excited because it meant dressing up, and I hadn't gone anywhere fancy in years. The strange thing was that Bob did not talk to me again about it for almost a month, and when the week before the big night rolled around and I hadn't heard from him, I thought that we really might not even be going. He finally showed up at my desk to remind me that the affair was that coming weekend, and I told him that I was upset that he hadn't talked to me in a month about it; I half revealed/half asserted that I hadn't bought a dress for the occasion. He said that he was sorry he hadn't approached me sooner about our date. He had been very busy and really wanted me to go, since he already had the tickets. He was hoping that I would still go with him and could borrow a dress or something. I accepted his apology and told him that I would get a dress somehow before the weekend.

Well, the evening finally came, and the first part of it went very well until half way through the night when Bob told me that the reason he had invited me to this shindig was that he had asked someone else and that first choice was not able to go. I was in shock and hurt. I couldn't understand why he would even tell me this, but then again, I hadn't been very honest with him about the fact that I was still dating Joe at the time. The beginning of our relationship definitely had its ups and downs, which would make another book in itself, but we finally put our cards on the table and told each other that we had been dating other people. Within a short time, I left Joe, and Bob left his girlfriend Debbie, and we began to date full-time.

I began to fall in love with this strange man.

He was certainly the opposite of my first husband; full of love for life, easy-going, funny, peaceful, and great to be around. We were married within a year after my first divorce, and I felt that my dreams were all coming true.

Bob and I started our lives in my little apartment in Northport, New York in February of 1975. A little less than one year later, in January '76 our first child was born. She was so beautiful: the perfect baby girl. We named her Holly, and she was the apple of her daddy's eye. In 1979, our son was born, and we named him Nicholas. As most parents do, we prayed that our children would always be happy and have a perfect life, never knowing then that one day our daughter would struggle with the knowledge that she had cancer.

Emotional exhaustion
Fills my very being.

I rush to work, to the store,
To get my errands done.

Laundry, yard work, bills, and more
Seem to be always waiting.

I vow that someday things will settle down and get easier.
Yet that day never seems to come.
I always feel like I am climbing mountains,
Hurrying to get to the top
Praying that I can see the rainbow
That lies on the other side of the hill.

But the mountain seems to get taller
The ground seems to get dryer
The trees don't seem to blossom any more
And I feel lost and alone.

I close my eyes and see a light

A light that has been waiting for me
A light that knows me, knows my soul, knows my very essence.

As I stare into this form
that grows
and becomes a crystalline snowflake,
I realize that for a moment
I have stopped climbing that mountain.
I have found inner peace
if only for a second.

I look around again
And see on a tree, that now has leaves
A perfect flower blooming.
This single living form
touching me,
expressing itself.

Have I been dashing through my life I ask…
from one minute to the next
Giving my all to the world
But yet not honoring my inner being?
The answer surprises me:

Yes, Dear One,
You have not stopped long enough
To allow yourself personal growth
For you feel in your heart that
Idleness is a waste of valued time.
You are so wrong!
Idleness is a time of great value.
It is a time for growth,

For connection with the universe
It is a time of being!

And so important to your soul
The soul which, for so long,
you have not honored.

Suddenly the rainbow appears
Its colors more vibrant and powerful
than those I have ever seen before
Time has stood still for one moment
And this moment has changed my life.

Chapter Seven

Rain drops fell. The sun's rays shined. Time glided on. Following the doctors' tentative consensus, Holly—no longer the infant of my reminiscing, but now an experienced young woman—was trying eagerly to get on with her life and to forget all that she had been through with her operation and cancer scare. I know that in the aftermath of the surgery, she frequently worried that the cancer would happen again. The surgery and the scare had changed her completely: She now had a new and deepened respect for her life and for the blessings that Life had given her. She became more spiritual, and she developed a great love for the world and the time she had in it. From those disturbing moments on, she always tried to make the most of her life.

I was so happy for Holly; but something deep inside me desperately wanted—perhaps even needed—to know if the reason that my daughter had developed the massive cancerous growth had something to do with my family medical history. Never before had I needed to know my background; I never cared quite as much, since in the beginning, the quest for my identity was only about me.   Now, my personal history involved my children and my children's health, and I was angry...and a little scared. I was determined to find out all that I could, not only to help Holly with what she had gone through, but also to be responsible to—and prepared for—my son and his future and my eventual grandchildren's future. What was this rare form of cancer that Holly had? Where did it come from? Was it genetic? Is there something we can do medically to safeguard Holly and to prevent an awful recurrence in our family?   I wanted answers, and I was going to find a way to get them.

The questions surrounding my genealogic background and why my daughter became ill circled relentlessly in my mind. How would I find out anything, where would I look, and where would I find the strength? Was there a strength inside me? (I had learned to be strong over the years, but I wondered... had I really?)

Remember: I had left high school feeling like I was worthless. My teachers' lack of warmth and encouragement had stolen the joy from my pursuit of the few subjects that I had done fairly well in. Recall: I only finished one year of college before I ran off to get married to my first husband and that marriage only lasted a little over one year. Consider: I suffered through a miscarriage and felt beaten down in so many ways, not only physically and emotionally, but spiritually too.

But, the good thing about remembering, recalling, and considering is that the memories are of times no longer with us; they are past, now soul memory, and are within us so that we can appreciate the progress of time in a positive way. I was able to use this appreciation of time's progress in a positive way: Just when I had surrendered all hope of learning what life was really about, I found love. True love. I had found Bob. I had made it through the worst and was looking forward to starting a real home with children where peace and love could abide.

A little to my surprise, the first few years of my second marriage were rough. I didn't realize how difficult it was to raise two children. Bob was working hard, and we had some tense ups and downs with how the kids should be raised. Bob had come from a very different family than I, and there were a few arguments that led us to pursue counseling. In the beginning of our marriage, I would wonder if this was the person to whom I really should be married for the rest of my life.

In retrospect, I am sure that many other couples have had this thought before. I can remember the arguments that went on, when I was a child, after my brother and I were in bed. My mother struggled with a lot of frustrating issues—stemming from her relationship with my dad. She was the 'go-getter' just like me, and my dad was the easy-going guy who wanted to take life slowly and evenly. My dad was very laid back, but there were times that were very stressful—especially when he would get laid off from his job. This happened at least three times that I can remember. As I mentioned, my dad built a darkroom in the house, for those times where he could bring in some extra money. However, as I indicated too, he was a very poor businessman and would barely earn enough money working on his own for all the work he would do.

The darkroom did come in handy though for one thing and that was hiding—or should I say hording—all the scissors, tape, staplers, paper clips and pens in the house. My mom—who knew that she possessed many such items—often couldn't find one of these items when she needed it. It wasn't long before she discovered that Dad kept them under lock-and-key in his downstairs sanctuary, the darkroom. Although my dad's space was a source of frustration on occasion for my mom, the room was a sanctuary for me. My dad did not mind me sitting with him and watching him work. It was a very special time for me and also one of the few one-on-one moments, in which I had my dad to myself.

Like my mom, I bore heavily taxing household responsibilities—with *my* husband, Bob, leaving in the morning and not coming home until late in the evening. He would come in the door at night and just relax. I certainly didn't expect my husband to be doing large projects in the evening, but sometimes it was hard for me to motivate him even to bring out the garbage. On the weekends, too, he would complain about having to do things around the house, and if I got him up to finally do something, he would be finding ways to take a break every few minutes. As far as having 'company,' guests, or visitors to our home, that work too was left up to me. So I took care of the kids, the house, the cooking, the laundry, the lawn, and the bills without too much complaining. I did wonder a few times if I had married Bob merely because he was so easy-going, the opposite of—and a life-affirming contrast to—my violent first husband; but I was learning about the flip side to being so easy-going. Maybe I should have waited longer between marriages for more of my own self-growth to occur, I thought, during those first years.

With time, however, Bob and I were able to communicate our feelings, which led to a greater understanding of each other's needs. Bob became more helpful around the house, and life became more joyful for me. As I grew spiritually, this energy spread and became part of Bob's life too, leading him to his own spiritual understanding and bringing us closer together over the years.

Our marriage has been a slow, but productive, process—a state-of-being in which love, understanding, and patience has endured and where it triumphs. This year, 2006, we will have been married 31 years. I can't say that it has always been easy, but I will say that we both have changed in many ways and that I love him with all of my heart. I feel that we have been two of the lucky ones. Although we have never been 'rolling in dough', we have always had a roof over our heads and food on the table. We have been truly blessed, and our lives have been made even more complete by having our children.

~

Because I developed toxemia while pregnant with our first child, Holly, I was placed in the hospital, where the doctors induced labor. Holly was born at 11:07PM on January 29th 1976, a few weeks early; she was supposed to be a February baby. She was everything I had hoped for, and Bob and I took pictures galore. She was a cautious child, and she didn't walk for fear of letting go, until she was 15 months old. Although she wasn't fond of bikes, skating, or anything where she didn't feel in control, she took dance lessons and became a beautiful dancer, which she continued to pursue throughout most of her life as a youth and even in college. Holly had been putting words on paper at 5 years old, and she would stay up evenings forming beautiful poems and stories that filled boxes in her closet.

Our son Nick was born three years after Holly, improbably also in the month of January, on the 24th 1979. He was a new loving energy in our family. He, different from Holly, started running around the house at eight months old. He was full of life, and wanted to be with his somewhat reluctant sister every second. When Nick was almost 2, we discovered why he, his dad, and I were always so frustrated trying to communicate with each other. The Eustachian tube that allowed fluids to drain from Nick's ear was too small to handle any congestion that Nick would experience. So when it was time for our son to learn to talk, he had trouble hearing the proper sounds that would help him pronounce the words that he needed to form sentences. Bob and I got him the help that he needed and also took him into the hospital to get tubes put in his ears. Although Nick struggled through his early school years, he hung in and years later graduated college with two degrees; one in astronomy and one in philosophy with a 3.7 average, all of this due to his determination and perseverance—traits that have accompanied him from young infancy to today.

My mom would try and help out now and then with our kids when the kids were young, but she would also say "You had them, so it is for you to take care of them." As a result of living this truth, it wasn't very often that Bob and I had time on our own. In fact, our first overnight get-away occurred when we had been married six years.

It was at that time when my mom said that she would watch the kids. She volunteered two days and one night. We were thrilled since she had never watched the kids before for more than a few hours. Holly was seven and Nick was four, not too young, but still a handful to take care of. I had spoken to Bob in advance about our possibly going to Pennsylvania. Although I wanted to make reservations at an inviting, romantic place, Bob felt that there was no need for reservations and was sure there would be many places to stay. My mom packed some wine, crackers and cheese for us and sent us on our way.

When we arrived in Lancaster, Pennsylvania we found that there were a few conventions in town and we couldn't find any vacancies. We ended up at the Visitors Center with many others who were looking for a place to stay. After about two hours, they came to us and told us that they would take us to a nearby house that had a cottage and was "just up the road a piece." I had heard that saying before and was a little nervous. After driving almost an hour, we got to our destination around 9:00PM. The owners seemed very nice as they showed us the cottage we were going to be staying in. We hadn't had dinner yet and asked the owners if there was a place to eat nearby. They said no, it was late and that everything was closed for the evening. We hoped there might be a movie theater nearby so that we could at least see a movie. The answer again was no, the closest theater was miles away. It certainly was not turning out to be the romantic get-a-way I had waited so long for.

Here, we were left to stay for the night. The cottage was dumpy looking: old furniture, cold tile floor, no closet, no TV, no phone and to add insult to injury, it was situated right next to a grave yard. I said to Bob that it was a good thing my mom had made us the little goodie box as I opened the wine, crackers, and cheese which became our dinner for the night. After eating, I told Bob that I was going to take a shower. I entered the bathroom to find there were no towels and asked Bob to please go to the main house to get some. I fumbled around with the shower knobs through the shower curtain to try and get the water going and set its temperature. Suddenly the water came on and I was soaking wet. The showerhead was pointing towards the toilet. I grabbed hold of the head and tried to turn it with no luck. I heard Bob coming back through the door and started screaming for him to come and help me. He could not make the showerhead move. So off the water went. I sponged myself off in the sink, wiped down the bathroom walls etc., tried to put a smile on my face, and stepped into the pretty lingerie I had bought especially for the trip. As I emerged from the bathroom, Bob was already in bed. He beckoned me to come to his side, and when I reached the bedside and looked down, I noticed that there was no mattress pad on the bed, only a thin sheet over the mattress. This turned my stomach, and I was about to say 'no-way am I getting into that bed,' when I heard a lawn mower start up. I said to myself "the owners couldn't be going to mow their lawn in the dark." Headlights on what was probably a large, ride-on mower came on. I sat down in the lounge chair by the bed and started to cry.

I couldn't believe what was happening. Bob tried to comfort me, but I was too angry about the situation and the fact that he hadn't made reservations in advance. A heated conversation followed for a long time, during all of which, the headlights and the man-on-the-mower went back and forth in front of our window. I reluctantly resigned myself to putting a bath towel on the bed and sleeping on it the whole night. The following morning we had to leave right after breakfast to get back home to my mom and the kids. As far as I was concerned, it was the weekend from Hell. Over the years, we have told this story many times, and—with the blunting and softening effects of time—it has finally become a source of laughter and enduring entertainment.

~

My mom took care of the kids that weekend without incident. She was tough. She had to be after my father had passed. Mom had already started in the business world and she had succeeded in making ends meet; thus, it was her path to continue as a working woman. It had been a hard life for her alone. Mom's family lived in Canada and was not close enough to assist her. My father's mother lived nearby, but the rest of the family lived miles away. I could feel what Mom was going through, and I did care, but we always seemed to have trouble communicating, so, although I saw my mother quite often, I tended to keep my distance emotionally.

The house that I grew up in, had, at one point, become too much for my mother to care for, and since she worked for a builder, Mario Bummara, she had his building company build a new house for her at cost. I was sad at the thought of my mom moving out of the house that I grew up in, but at the time that it occurred, I was living in Germany with my first husband. I was aware that my mom had to move for financial reasons, and since I had left home without telling her, certainly I had no say in the matter.

Not long after the move, my mom was hoping that my grandmother (my father's mother)—who was alone and not in the best of health—would move in with her. Mom's plan was to have the house built, live in the first two levels of this new house, and have my grandmother live upstairs in the apartment to be built, where my mom could take care of grandma. My grandmother would have all the conveniences, use of the yard, and a private entrance. When my mom suggested this idea to my Uncle Cam (my father's brother) and his wife, my Aunt Carol, they told my mom that they would take care of grandma instead, since they thought it best not to burden my mother with grandma's problems. They decided that they would put my grandmother into a nursing home in New Jersey, near them. My mom was hurt and upset with them and could not really understand why they did not want her to take care of my grandmother, but the apartment was already in the making, and she couldn't turn back now. [Over the years, mom was lucky to find some very special people to live there. To this day, we remain friends with one couple from Switzerland who lived in my mom's house. My mom became so close to them: we spent many holidays together; they even made my mom the godmother to their second child.]

The day that it was time to move my grandmother out of her home in Levittown, Long Island, my mother went to grandma's house to help, but when she got there, mostly everything had been taken care of. She was shocked that my aunt and uncle had done so much without her. Even now, I am not totally sure what happened between my mom and my aunt and uncle, but things went from bad to worse. On that day, they had words between them, and their relationship ended entirely.   (There had been several past scuffles between mom and Aunt Carol & Uncle Cam. The most significant: shortly after Dad died, mom wanted to go alone to bury his ashes; she told my aunt and uncle not to come to the cemetery.   This caused what may have been an irreversible rift.)

I was a grown, married adult when this separation occurred and was just beginning to feel close to my Aunt Carol and Uncle Cam, and now my mom was trumpeting how upset she was with the situation and that she didn't want *me* to see them anymore. Bob and I tried to encourage the feuding family to talk to each other, but our efforts were futile.   Another hill for me to climb, for I couldn't completely understand why this was happening. Why was my mother so controlling, domineering, and overprotective? She felt that my aunt and uncle were not good people, and she did not want me to have anything to do with them. I had grown up my whole life knowing this part of the family. They were the only real extended family I had ever known. I wanted to still see my aunt and uncle, but didn't know what to do. My mother was a powerful force, and although I tried to prevent this family separation, she made me feel that I would be disrespecting her if I saw the two. My aunt and uncle also knew of my mother's strength and did not want to interfere or cause any more problems. I secretly continued speaking to my aunt and uncle on the phone, but hated keeping it a secret from my mom. My aunt and uncle did not want to push me. They knew the situation, how my mother was, and they told me that they would honor my decision and my wishes. My mother had disappointed me again and I felt hurt, afraid, and alone.

It took over three years before I finally got the nerve to go and see my Aunt Carol and Uncle Cam, without my mother knowing. I can remember after thirty-six months, seeing my uncle again for the first time. He held me in his arms, and tears came to his eyes. I too was crying and looked up at him and said, "It is so nice to see you again. I know my farther would have wanted this too." Yes, my father who loved everyone, would never have wanted a separation. He loved his brother and would have wanted us to be together always.

I think about the devastation, depression, abandonment, fear, and resentment that families put themselves through over misunderstandings, confusion, mistrust, and jealousy. Why do we as humans isolate ourselves from our loved ones and from the people who have always been such a close part of our lives? Why do small issues turn into big ones and end in never speaking to a loved one again? These things were so hard for me to understand and accept. I didn't want to accept them; I wanted a family, any family, and for some reason I had to fight for any family I could get.

~

During the time that my children were growing, I was growing with them. I wanted to try something on my own, something that was for me, for a change. I had given myself to my first husband, given myself to my second, given myself to my children, but had never given myself to myself.

I really thought that to be a good person was to do for others. After all, I was taught that if you do good work, you will be rewarded in heaven. There was nothing I had learned in church about taking care of oneself—such self-attention was far too <u>selfish</u>, for heaven's sake! Even though I knew that I needed some time for myself, I felt guilty about taking it. I felt guilty about even sitting down to rest, sitting to read a book. How wasteful could your life be, or you be to others, if all you did was sit. My mind would run constantly—inventing things I needed to do, but I never noticed how much I was running myself into the ground. After all, I had a lot of responsibility: a husband, children, a dog, and a house. I really don't think that I would have even gone looking for a dance class if it weren't for the fact that I was tired of being home and just wanted to escape. I wish that I had fully realized then how important it is for a person to just Be: the value of meditation, living in the moment, recognizing your own self-worth. I look back now and see how much better a parent and wife I could have been if I would have really worked at appreciating myself and been able to let go of the guilt I felt in doing for myself.

I got brave enough to talk to someone who allowed me to try an advanced dance class. I did very well in it (even I felt assured). I became/discovered that I was an adept dancer despite the small number of lessons. I felt as if I knew how to read without actually knowing the alphabet. After a few years of lessons, I was quite a good dancer, and the opportunity came up for me to teach a class, which was something I thought I could do. I was a little nervous about it, but loved children and felt I could teach them with warmth, compassion, and love, conditions that I felt were lacking in most dance studios.

The director of the studio where I was taking lessons had hurt herself, and everyone needed to shift positions to make the studio function properly.

One lady who was teaching had to give up her class in one of the local elementary schools in order to fill in at the dance studio. She asked me if I wanted to take over her elementary school class. I said yes, of course, since it was only going to be one hour long, once a week. I did not know at the time that this seemingly random turn of events would turn out to be a new beginning for me, and one of the most important parts of my life.

The kids and parents at the school loved me so much as a teacher that not only did the school ask me to come back and teach more, but very soon the parents were asking if I had my own studio: they wanted private classes and lessons for their children. My confidence was finally beginning to grow.

I couldn't believe that people were interested in me teaching their children, but how could I run my own studio, where would I do it, and most importantly what about my family, which in my mind came first? Holly was only eight years old and Nick was five. He was struggling with school, and I wanted to be there for both of them when they got home; I wanted to help them with their homework, make dinner, and put them to bed. I knew Bob would help me somewhat, but he wouldn't be home until dinner time. What would happen in-between? If I had my own studio, the classes would need to start around 3:00PM (because my students-to-be were at school during the day) and the classes might not end till 9:00PM. And what about building a dance studio without even having any definite students? Were Bob and I willing to take that chance?

I knew that I had to think about it, and think about it I did for <u>three</u> years while I continued to run the after-school dance classes. Finally, I felt that my own children might be old enough to take care of themselves, and I had been smart enough to collect the names of my students from the elementary school over the years. So with the little money that I had saved, and the help of a very dear friend, I changed my garage into a dance studio. I remember laughing and telling Bob that if things didn't work out and I didn't get any students who were really interested in coming to dance, at least we would have a beautiful den.

As it turned out, the dance studio opened in September 1987 with 27 students. I was in heaven. I was even able to make my own children their dinner in advance: they could easily put it into the microwave and heat it up. This blessing kept my guilt down to a minimum.

Yes guilt—there was a lot of that in my life. Since I lacked confidence in myself and frequently felt that nothing I did was good enough, almost every situation presented me with a rough road of many lessons to learn. I learned from my hardships in school; I learned from going through my first divorce; and I learned from my father's death. Too bad I really didn't see how much these things really were helping me grow. When my children were little, I could only look back and say that I had a hard life and I was going to make their lives better. I would give them everything that I didn't have, I told myself. How silly I was; how long would that last?

I had heard that the first few years of your child's life are really the most important. Oh how true this is: for we as parents, we instill in them most of what they know before they start school. I firmly know this now. I had to learn that although Holly and Nick were the most important things in my life, I wasn't always going to be the most important thing to them. Yes—all children like mine would grow up and become adults, and we as parents cannot protect them from disappointment, pain, sorrow, or sadness. We each come to this earth to experience these feelings and emotions, which hopefully in the long run, bring us closer to why we have come here in the first place, with the understanding of a higher Creator and love of the Divine.

It was during the second year of teaching in my dance studio that I met a beautiful family called the Moons. They had a 6-year-old daughter named Deanna who wanted to dance, and I took her under my wing and watched her grow into a young woman over the next few years. She was a quiet, loving, caring, and beautiful child who gave me no problems in class, unlike some of my other students. It was a pleasure teaching her and she practiced hard to learn every new dance step she was given. I became very close to her family, which was not the usual, and her mom and I would spend time on the phone just talking about life.

Deanna had been dancing with me for 3 years when, on one March day, my son came running through the front door after school to tell me that Deanna had been strangled by the gym door and was in the hospital in a coma. I couldn't believe my ears. I had just seen her a few days before and could remember looking at her and saying to myself how beautiful she was and how much she had grown.

She passed 10 days later on March 23rd, 1991 at North Shore Hospital on Long Island. This young child had touched the hearts of all who met her, and we were devastated and shocked that God had taken her.

[The particulars of the accident were tragic. The safety device on the sliding gym door had been malfunctioning for years. This was the piece that would make the door retract back away from any object that might come in contact with the door while it was closing—in a way similar to closing elevator or subway doors. The gym door also had a switch that was supposed to be hand-held by someone who might be opening or closing the door. Over the years, since this door closed and opened very slowly—except for the last section which would snap closed to lock—the gym teachers between classes had been shown how to jam the switch, so they could take care of the kids, making sure they were changing clothes for their next class. In the case of Deanna, what happened was: class had been dismissed and the gym teacher had jammed the switch and gone into the locker room to take care of the kids. All the children were with their regular school teachers, and Deanna asked hers if she and her two friends could get a drink. The teacher said yes. The girls had been on the boys' side of the gym and without the teacher knowing, the girls decided that they would get their drink from the girls' side of the gym where there were no boy cooties. The girls left the teacher and ran around the outside of the gym to get their drink. On the way back, in order to save time and get back to their class, they decided to cross through the gym. The doors were in motion, and Deanna's two friends ran past the closing door. As Deanna went through, her headband fell off, and as she reached down to pick it up, the last door snapped shut on her neck holding her there between the door and the wall. The door would not retract back because the safety device was broken. The girl's screams sent the teachers running, and the fire department that was right next door arrived in minutes. They used the "jaws of life," but it took them far too long to release the door from Deanna's neck. It was too late: the damage had been done. They air-lifted the little girl to North Shore Hospital on Long Island. The doctors did all they could.]

This event affected hundreds of families in the Huntington area. People were bewildered about what had happened and were talking about it for weeks and years. The issue of negligence cast a shadow with great reach. A school that needed roof repairs closed down toward the end of that year, and people not knowing the school's situation blamed the closure on what had happened to Deanna.

The news of Deanna's death hit my son Nicholas really hard. He really liked the gym teacher that was involved and had developed a lot of respect for him. He also had grown close to Deanna's family, over the years seeing them every week at the dance studio. His feelings were split, and he did not know what to think or whom to blame—if anyone—for Deanna's death. Our family spent a lot of time talking with him, for we too had to work through the devastation, sorrow, and emotional confusion of this horrific situation.

Many years have gone by since this mind-numbing event, and Deanna's parents and sister have found the strength to go on. With Deanna's inspiration from above, they were able to help pass a law that protects children from having similar accidents from happening to them. The Moon family knows that Deanna has guided them through all of their endeavors, and she continues to follow and help them daily through and with their own personal lives.

We all miss Deanna's beautiful smile and love for life, but we know that others have been helped by her soul's strength to come into this world to improve it in many ways. Since her death, each year, the "Deanna Memorial Award" is given in her honor, to one student who has shown the most improvement during the year in dance at my studio. The children know that it is a special honor to receive this award, and they have their names placed on a plaque in the dance studio.

~

Deanna's death reinforced my own natural urge to improve my children's lives while I was still here, on this earth, in part by giving them the information of who they are and where they came from. As you know, with the eventual cooperation and help of my mom, I learned that my birth name appeared in black and white on some very real adoption papers: "Kathy Jane Segur." Much time had passed since my mother's reluctant cooperation/revelation and I still wondered, what kind of a name is "Segur?" I had no idea what nationality it was. A few of my friends guessed at what my background might be, but no one knew for sure. I asked them if they had any ideas about doing a search on the Internet, and they gave me a few ideas about where to start the search. Months went by with no luck as I registered with different adoption agencies that I had hoped could help me, but no results.

I finally received minimal information from the New York State Department of Health. It was from the Adoption Information Registry division. The document was entitled "Non-identifying Information Report." The title basically said it all. The report told me my mother was white, 24 years old when she had me, Protestant; it was a normal pregnancy, and my father had abandoned her prior to birth. There was nothing at all about my health history which was what I was mainly looking for. It didn't even say anything about my birth name, which by now, I had already known from the adoption paperwork. The most important information was that the adoption was handled by Wayne County Department of Social Services in New York, which I immediately wrote with no luck. Most other relevant organizations told me they couldn't give me any information, since my birth records had been sealed.

I remind you that I wrote over a hundred letters pleading my case to different legislators. I remind you that only a few answered and told me that there was nothing they could do to help me. I learned with no sympathy that since my birth records had been sealed, they could only be opened in the case of a medical emergency, and in that case, I would have to go to court. I found that law to be especially stupid because if someone was in a real emergency, who would have the time or strength to go to court?! I certainly was not in a position to afford a lawyer and try to fight personally something that others in New York State had already been doing for years.

I was about to give up hope.

I did not know what to do.

I redoubled my online efforts and launched a major new search to find the name Segur on the Internet. I searched all types of sites: from social security to death registries, local addresses to national. I found the name Segur more than once, and was happy—in a way—not to see very many listed. I rejoiced in finding that Segur isn't particularly common, and I hoped that my name's scarcity would help me narrow the search. Since I lived in New York, I was hoping that the adoption agency (whomever they were) hadn't shipped me as a child very far from home. I was brought up on Long Island and born in Rochester, New York, so I hoped that if there were some Segurs in New York, I might have a chance. There were a few names listed here and also some down south, including in Florida. Well that was all well and good, except now that I had the names, what could I do? I knew the most important thing to me was medical history; it was just a matter of figuring out what to say to these people to get it, especially since I didn't even know if they were my family.

I composed a letter pleading with anyone who received it to answer me. Explaining the situation of my daughter and her rare form of cancer, I emphasized the critical need to give my daughter's doctors a reliable medical family history. I didn't know if anything would happen, but I sent out 24 letters to all of the Segur families that I could find on the East Coast. I also did a lot of praying. I wanted to help my daughter and my son to find their family history. As much as helping their physical health, I wanted to contribute to their psychological well-being: I knew first-hand how isolated a person feels when the doctor asks the standard question "Any family history" and that person says "Your guess is as good as mine."

Not knowing anything about your real family is a strange feeling. You wonder if there is someone out there who looks like you, acts like you, and has similar traits. I had experienced first-hand what positive thinking could do and how I could manifest good in my life. I was becoming a more understanding, more positive-thinking person. I had already been through so much, and it was time not only for Holly to heal, but time for me as well. I had done all that I could to help her, I felt, and when I walked the letters to the mail box, and put them in, I asked God to grant me what I was seeking, if it was for my highest good. Either way, I knew I had lived through my life without any knowledge of my real family, and I knew that my kids could too if that is how the Universe chose to unfold. I had taught my kids to be strong, and they had both overcome amazing obstacles.

So off the letters went, on September 30, 1999, me having no idea where they would end up or if I would ever even hear anything. My job was done. It was time for me to rest. Our family life began to get back to normal, with the exception of me appreciating them even more. I treasured my time with each of them: with my husband Bob, with Holly, and with my son Nick. I have to admit I worried about Holly most, praying that the horror she had gone through would never return.

~

Time and the sequence of events in one's life have a way of playing games with the mind. The seemingly linear "before" and "after" of our day-to-day existence often—in the perception of our Soul—appears majestically circular, with no objective beginning or end, no definitive "pre-" or "post-" sequencing, no "real" order of events in which they "actually" happened. Recognizing such infinity is one of the beauties of seeing time, with newly aware eyes, as a convenient construction that we have Created to facilitate our joy.

And so (somewhere in the continuum), once Holly was better and back working at Hallmark, she and Bill were able to save enough money to get an apartment on their own. Bob and I were so happy for them, seeing them beginning to start their lives over again without any worries. After the manager of Hallmark left, Holly was able to take over the manager's position, earning a little more money to aid paying the bills from her hospital stay. It was hard; Holly and Bill had been through a lot; yet they seemed happy.

Nick started college at Farmingdale. Since he never liked high school, we were delighted and surprised that he wanted to go to college. He started out taking general subjects and then tried and found something he loved: astronomy. He did very well and was able to get into Stony Brook University the following year, continuing his interest not only in astronomy, but also in philosophy.

Bob was still working in New York working for a company called Cox and Co., an anti-icing and de-icing electronic heater manufacturer, as a product assurance test engineer. He loved his job. This made the long day and the hours of travel more bearable. He got more involved in his hobby of collecting American coins and would spend hours on the train or at home reading about the subject. He eventually knew more than the average coin dealer and collector and began giving people coin estimates and guided them or helped them invest in coins of more value. To this day, he gets great pleasure out of doing this, and has had his name printed in coin books, and advertised in coin magazines.

I continued my work with the dance studio, my student enrollment growing every year. By 1992, I had about 35 students. I had met many wonderful children and people during that time, and my confidence and complete sense of myself continued to grow.

I had one student whose name was strangely enough Holly, the same as my daughter. The name was not that common on Long Island, and I was surprised when I first heard her name spelled the same way, and not short for Hollace. Her mother Jayne was very nice, and we would chat whenever she and her daughter would come into the studio. We not only became very good friends, but Jayne also began taking dance lessons from me. As I got to know her, I found out that Jayne too was interested in a more spiritual approach to life. She belonged to a spiritual group and told me that I should come with her sometime and meet the people. I went one evening, and found the participants all to be very kind. They were a metaphysical study group who called themselves "The L.O.V.E. Center." The initials stood for: Learning, Oneness, Victorious, Enlightenment. I would go there with her whenever I could, but it was difficult with the dance studio, since both activities went on in the evening.

Quite a few years went by, and I was being drawn more and more to the spiritual side of life. My daughter, too, had answered the call and had started her own spiritual woman's circle group with her friends. She spoke to me about it often and how much she and her friends had grown from it. I was very intrigued and thought about starting my own group. I spoke to Jayne about my daughter's group and asked her if she wanted to start one with me. She said 'yes,' and in no time, we had a small group of women who would gather together at someone's house once a month. The group taught me how to express myself and how to interact with other adults. After all, I was very isolated in that area, working mainly with children through the dance studio and not getting out much socially. Although I had done so many things in my life, I was still a very shy person.

Isn't it funny how we meet so many people in our lives, each with his or her own gifts, personality, and appearance. Yet do we really know them, or what they have been through? I always felt that most people were better than me in so many ways, never realizing that each of us struggles inside with personal issues, and that no one except maybe our best friends might know who we really are. We don't want to express these feelings to anyone, in fear of what others might say or how we might be judged. Fear is such a debilitating illness.

Our women's circle met once a month for about four years. We called ourselves "The Daughters of the Moon Dove," a name that was chosen by vote from the many ideas that the women creatively brought to our earliest gatherings. (We invented the image and creature of a "Moon Dove" as an informal merging of themes: loosely honoring the peace of the dove and the nighttime beauty & tranquility of the moon. Very often our meetings were held peacefully at night.)

The group supported each of us in ways that we never completely expressed. You see, even in the seemingly safe environment of that group, there were some fears and concerns of sharing freely. On that rare occasion when someone felt comfortable enough to express themselves, the true expression of what we meant to each other was momentarily uttered. I found much love and support, being with these women, and found myself wanting to open up to the love and compassion they too wanted to give.

But a big question lingered: was I strong enough to fully let go?

Across the chasms and journeys of time
the followers are with us

They guide our moves
they guide our essence

They protect and nurture us
They are here to
keep us whole,
Safe,
Renewed

Their passions are great
and as strong as ours
In some ways, even stronger

They want more for us
More than we can imagine,
For they know our true Self
Our true essence

We have come through eons of time
and space

practicing and perceiving
who we are

When we start each incarnation,
we learn what we believe to be right,
not touching our inner being
which already knows our truth

Suddenly, we sense our soul's essence!
We begin to know our life's purpose
our life's truth
We find that we fit into many dimensions

The dimension known as earth
is just a fragment of the
All that Is
For there are many dimensions
and we are ONE with ALL
Unified and Whole

Chapter Eight

Compassion: something we all need and something I so wanted from my parents. My father was gone, and I felt my mother's heart longing to be close to me, but somehow neither of us knew how to be close. I wondered if our recent opening and sharing—as adults—of the adoption papers would be what we needed to clear the air and bring us closer together.

It wasn't: The block still remained.

My feelings for my mother were changing in a helpful way though, and I was beginning to let go of the need that I thought I had for a perfect relationship with my mom. I was starting a new journey now: a journey of realizations, including the realization that someone and something was deeply missing in my life, and that someone was not my father who had passed away; it was not my mother, who was sometimes emotionally distant, and it was not any man or romantic love. The someone sorely missing in my life was... ME. The ME who I had not taken the time to truly know, the soul ME, the inner me, the lost ME, for whom I was searching and had not yet found.

Holly's ordeal had led me to seek my own personal completion. The rude awakening of how short life can be and its possible ending without the spiritual growth and understanding of why we came to this earth in the first place, penetrated me to the foundation of my being.

Holly found another facet of this same sentiment deep within her heart and shared her feelings with me when she wrote the following letter, shortly after her confrontation with cancer.

January 30th 1999

Dear Mom and Dad,

A little over a year ago, I prayed and wished that I could reach my 22nd birthday. And now I am 23!! Sometimes, as much as it may seem like a simple thing to have birthdays, I realize how much more birthdays mean to me.

Thank you Mom and Dad for making my 23rd birthday wonderful and for your support and undying love in keeping me and "my life" even more wonderful! Without the two of you, I would not have had anyone to base my kindness, love and happiness on! Basically, thank you for being two great role models in my life.

Love you, Holly

The *whole* family was grateful even beyond soul-level ecstasy that Holly had survived this ordeal with cancer and now had more time to live her life, time to make the most of each moment, and time to discover the new meaning of life with God's strength. I routinely prayed that God would watch over Holly and give her the courage to fulfill her dreams. This visioning that I did also contained my own personal prayer: including a renewed commitment to living my life to the fullest, to making something out of it, and to following my own most deeply held dreams.

The dance studio had fulfilled a (sometimes unspoken) dream that I had carried and held dear since I was a little girl. I had long thought that by fulfilling this dream I would find some completion; I instead found something still missing inside me. I found the notion of this void hard to understand. How could my dream of dancing and owning my own studio come true, and yet there <u>still</u> be something missing?

I was learning that there are many things in life, which we desire, that we <u>think</u> will <u>complete</u> us, but we are often blinded to the fact that the true reason that we are here is not to fulfill the dreams that we may <u>think</u> we desire, but instead to complete the true inner growth of our soul, which is the biggest part of who we truly are. We as humans tend to ignore (or fail to understand or believe in) our own <u>souls</u> with which we came into this life; each of our unique souls has wanted to touch us and complete us in some way. How can we expect to feel complete if we do not allow our mental and spiritual sides to <u>blend</u> together? Do we take the time to learn more about ourselves, read about personal intuitive growth, give ourselves time to meditate, and—perhaps most neglected of all—trust and honor our spiritual side? Becoming <u>conscious</u> and <u>aware</u> is how we begin to integrate and blend, and I was just learning how to recognize and honor the soul part of me. I was beginning to let my soul emerge and bring joy and happiness to a heart that was aching inside.

Each year, as owner/manager of the dance studio, I would acquire a few more new students. It was wonderful to see the venue expanding, and I just loved the little ones and enjoyed watching them grow into adults. How blessed I was to be working with each one of them and touching their lives in some way. I wanted each year to be better than the one before, and I continued to try and out-perform myself. Before I was even done with one year's recital I was thinking about a theme for the next. My mind never stopped working: between the choreography, costumes, stage design and paper work, I was constantly busy. Yes: the studio was growing and I was happy; but, the whole effort was taking up so (too) much of my time and becoming a bigger and bigger part of my life.

More often than not, my studio work was very enjoyable, and I frequently felt that I had found my purpose and niche in life. Yet there were still moments in which I felt my strong and independent nature faltering, bringing me back to an intermittent frightening reality that life hadn't quite changed for me all that much.

Reflecting on one of those times involving my mom, I can still remember the sudden disappearance of the love and respect that I so desperately [thought I] needed. The love seemed to escape just past my grasp. The ordeal started one Thursday evening during the second year of my dance studio's dress rehearsal, in June 1989. The kids and two adults were performing their final routine (the finale) and I looked on with such pride in my heart. When the performance ended, my mom—who had come there to help me—approached the edge of the stage. In front of all the kids on the stage and their parents who were in the audience, she said, "I think you really need to do something about that number. It looks terrible since Terry's body is blocking a lot of the kids in that one section where you are forming a circle." (Terry was my friend and one of the adults.)

I valued my mother's opinion, and so I brought the kids out on stage to do the number again, trying to change the movement, position, and timing of the number. The efforts didn't work, and the kids went off the stage crying. I told them not to worry about it; we would leave it alone: it was going to be all right. Terry was mortified, and she too didn't know what to say or do. My mom was insistent and wanted to know how I was going to fix the problem. I told her there was nothing that I could do about it at the time. The recital was the <u>next day</u>, and an incident which should have been short-lived and small turned into a major problem. My mother badgered me all night, wanting to know what I was going to do. I wanted the show to be perfect; I didn't want to upset the kids; I didn't really want to change the number; I didn't feel it was that bad, but maybe my mother was right. I tossed and turned all night worrying about how I could fix the number. At the time, I did not realize that it was my own inner demon rearing its ugly head again: It was my own sense of worthlessness and my determination to prove to my mother my love for her that was driving me to this state of inner turmoil.

I spoke to my friend Terry the next morning and told her that when she and the other adult, Elaine, got on stage they could attempt to hold the kids back by walking more slowly, so that she and Elaine would finish/remain on the sides of the stage—not in the front—and clear of blocking any child in any way. I did not tell my mother what I was doing or that I hadn't slept due to her comments. The recital came. Terry and Elaine slowed down their steps, and the plan worked perfectly. However, I felt deeply that my mom had over-stepped her bounds by aggressively advising me in front of all the people. I wanted to talk to her, but like so many times before, I was afraid to confront her with the situation.

Finally, about a month later, on her birthday, I decided to bring up my feelings on the subject. I had learned to express myself tactfully over the years. The careful use of language was my way of trying to protect myself from confrontations. I told my mom as tactfully as I could that I appreciated her help and valued her opinion, but I would have preferred that she had expressed her feelings to me at the dress rehearsal on the side and not in front of all the children and their parents.

She flipped out!

She started yelling at me. She said that if I didn't want her help, why didn't I just say so. The next 45 minutes were pure hell. I kept trying to explain calmly to her that I did want her help, but that I would have just appreciated her delivering the help in a more private and constructive manner. She yelled back, and screamed, "After all I have tried to do for you, this is what you say to me."

I tried over and over again to remain calm and explain; all the while Bob and my daughter stood by, saying nothing.

I finally couldn't take it any longer, and I lost it. I pick up the kitchen chair and threw it violently on the floor, screaming at my mother that no matter what I did or said, she would never understand me. I turned around and ran out of the house with no shoes on. To this day, I don't know how I got half a mile down the road in a minute. I ran and cried and ran and cried until I could go no more. I didn't want to see her again, and I didn't want to go back to the house. My daughter had run outside, out of concern, to find me, but she could not see me anywhere. Finally, after about a half hour, I calmed down enough again to come back home. My mom had left. I felt guilt that I had spoiled her birthday and blamed myself for the bad timing and the situation. We did eventually talk again. But as usual, I apologized for something I feel I really shouldn't have had to. But this was my mom; this was me; and this was how we were living our lives in that moment.

The strength that I thought I had developed from running my own business seemed to be a farce, since my old childhood insecurities kept coming back to haunt me. I needed to find a better way not only to deal with my mom, but also to handle other situations and challenging people that kept coming into my life. I was healing and moving forward, trying to create balance, but the process seemed so slow that progress was barely recognizable to me.

My friend Jayne and I continued to go to the L.O.V.E. Center, where the group spoke of many different spiritual notions. Some of these notions I had already personally experienced and had been interested in for a long time. It was wonderful to be with Jayne and a great blessing to finally have someone like her in my life, a real friend with whom I could talk. I already knew that I was in a very different place than the people in my family and church: as I have said before, I've frequently felt that there was something much more profound out there for me to discover. Dreams, in the many senses of the word, were a part of that feeling for me.

~

Alice Didier, who was a friend of my mom's, knew that I had written down some of my nighttime dreams in the past, but I never really took the time to understand their meaning or how they could help my everyday life. Alice had spent quite a few years journaling her own dreams and found them, once studied, to give great understanding in her life. She was kind enough to give me some ideas on how to organize and journal my own dreams. She taught me how to study their hidden meanings and clues. I was soon reading many books on the subject, which taught me even more about dreamwork.

Although I haven't discussed it much, my dreams—as I was growing up—had always been a source of guidance for me, whenever I would need help, and I knew that if I could understand my dreams, I would receive more spiritual insight.

I had already experienced how dreams could be somewhat profound at times, but when I started to organize them and pay attention, I not only noticed that I could remember them better, but I discovered how much they could help me in my daily life. This was especially prevalent with my dance studio work involving my creativity. I would often literally dream up stage designs that I then would physically create.

One time that stands out in my memory was the year that I was doing some songs from Walt Disney. The opening number of the show was the "Electric Light Parade." I had seen the actual parade in Florida at Disney World, and it was beautiful with all the floats and even the people decked out in lights. I thought to myself: wouldn't it be wonderful if I could place my dance students in the opening number in lighted costumes. But how could I do that? The battery packs alone cost a fortune and were too heavy for the children to carry. My mind searched the different possible ways that this could be done, but none of them were practical or would *really work. One night, when I could think about it no more, I went to bed asking God to help me. Lo and behold I had an amazing dream. I saw the children with a string of lights down their arms, each lit, and as the kids maneuvered their arms up and down, from one position to the next, they created many beautiful lighted formations. I woke up with so much excitement and thanked God for giving me this wonderful idea. Later that week, in the life we call 'reality,' I took strings of <u>illuminated</u> bulbs (Christmas lights!) and velcroed them to the material covering the shoulders of the children. The parade of linear luminescence was safely plugged into an outlet at the side of the stage. The children were able to showcase the light string by holding hands: The whole group could then move their arms in different ways, creating interesting light formations. [I could write a whole book on the creative ideas that Spirit has given me when I would just take the time to reach out and recognize their messages.]*

Jayne and I began to talk about the many experiences we had had while growing up. These experiences involved unexplainable events in our lives that occurred through dreams, 'miracles', seeing, hearing, smelling and just knowing unexplainable phenomena. The field was fascinating to me and she encouraged me to read many books on these subjects.

As I read, I became more and more interested in my own spirituality. It felt right to me, and the books that I chose answered many questions that I had in a loving and fulfilling way. I began to sense that maybe there was some hope for me in God's eyes, that in fact, He wasn't this terrible energy that I had *learned to fear as a child. He was love, and in fact, since we were a part of <u>Him</u>, we were love too, made from His pure essence.*

~

By the spring of 1999, life had pretty much gone back to normal, and Holly had made progress in her job. When her boss left, she was promoted to manager, and Holly seemed very happy at first with the new position, even though it didn't offer more money. After a while, the stress started to catch up to her again, and she found herself looking for another job that would be more relaxing and that would—hopefully—offer her more money. She ended up at another greeting card store in the town of Huntington.

I was a little concerned about all of the pressure that my daughter was under, and time was drawing nearer for her to go for her first regular CAT scan. When I asked her if she had made her appointment, she said no, that she felt all right, and would make it sometime soon. I hung up the phone thinking that although she had said she felt fine, she hadn't felt much of anything last time when the cyst had grown so quickly in just a few months and became 15 inches in size. I didn't want to see this happen to her again. I tried to encourage her to make her doctor's appointment at the end of the current six-month period, which is when they told her she should go for her test. I wondered if the reason she was being so aloof was because she really didn't want to know. I wasn't sure, but I was truly concerned and prayed that she would do the right thing.

Yes—there are times that caring for someone, especially a child, can be hard. She wasn't a little girl anymore; she was 23 years old and a married woman. I certainly didn't want to nag at her all the time. Yet this was my child, and I wanted to keep her safe. This wasn't a small thing we were talking about; this was her life and infinitely important. I said my piece once or twice, and when she didn't move on my advice right away, I prayed to God that she would do the right thing and be all right.

The year 1999 ended; the new year had begun, and it wasn't going to be long before it would be June 2000. Holly and I had talked about doing a dance together for the June recital and picked the song "The Prayer" by Celine Dion, from the movie "Quest for Camelot." We practiced throughout the first part of the year and when the audience watched us dance in June at the recital, there wasn't a dry eye in the house. They all knew what we had been through during the past year with Holly's health, and the words of the song touched not only our hearts but also the hearts of all the people who watched. I would like to enter the words of the song here to show the feeling and renewed respect and love for life and guidance that Holly and I both felt.

"The Prayer" by Celine Dion

I pray you'll be my eyes
And watch her where she goes
And help her to be wise
Help me to let go
Every mother's prayer
Every child knows
Lead her to a place
Guide her with your grace
To a place where she'll be safe
I pray she finds your light

And holds it in her heart
As darkness falls each night
Remind her where you are
Every mother's prayer
Every child knows
Need to find a place
Guide her to a place
Give her faith so she'll be safe
Lead her to a place
Guide her with your grace
To a place where she'll be safe

I tried to focus my mind on all of the beautiful blessings that I had in my life: a wonderful job, family, and good health for everyone in it at this time. I worked hard on every detail of the dance studio's needs, trying to keep my mind on only positive thoughts; then the day finally came: Holly told me that she was going for her first CAT scan; I was so happy. I had tried to pretend that it didn't matter whether I knew for sure if my daughter's health was holding up, but the bottom line was, I really just needed to know.

The results of the CAT scan came back:

Holly was in good health. I thanked God with all of my being. The doctor had said that we could feel pretty secure that the cancer was truly gone once she made it through four years of good health, and we had now just finished the first. I hated the idea of waiting and wondering from one scan to the next and prayed that I would find out my past health history or get an answer from one of my possible birth families, the people to whom I had sent letters.

~

I was growing more and more impatient as the year ticked by, wondering if I would ever hear from any family member. My meditations and prayers helped my strength, and I continued doing my spiritual work, becoming stronger and spending more time with Jayne, the L.O.V.E. Center, and Women's Circle. Reading books on spirituality became an important part of my life, and each new day brought many empowering experiences. Here are just a few of the books I enjoyed: *Many Lives Many Masters* by Brian L. Weiss, M.D.; *The Seven Spiritual Laws of Success* by Deepak Chopra; *You Can Heal Your Body* by Louise L. Hay; *The Four Agreements* by Don Miguel Ruiz; *Excuse Me, Your Life Is Waiting* by Lynn Grabhorn; and *Love And Power* by Lynn V. Andrews. I also read most of Ted Andrews' books, and one of my favorite authors at the time was Sylvia Browne.

I was finally beginning to become my own person. There was an increasingly stabilizing sense within me that made me feel 'maybe I'll really be all right'. Seeing the results of the recital and all my hard work gave me inner confidence that I didn't have before. It was really hard work, and for most of it, I received no financial compensation. This didn't matter to me because my main reason for running the dance studio was to give of myself to others, and to create a home-like, family environment. The small amount of revenue that I brought in barely covered my expenses, and many of my friends couldn't understand why I was even doing it. I often explained that if it was just about the money, I wouldn't be involved with the studio in any way. It was about me, about me doing something I've always wanted to do, about giving to others, and about fulfilling a childhood dream and expressing my creativity. But beyond all that, Spirit knew it was time for me to discover my soul essence, who I truly was.

There were many lessons as I ran my own dance studio, and I made my share of mistakes, always coming out on top with renewed fortitude and courage. Each year, things improved, and so did my dealing with people. Most people loved the type of homey environment that I offered; many knew where I was coming from and what I was trying to do. Some must have thought I had it real easy with all the money they thought I was collecting in only two days of work. They never considered the time involved in ordering the costumes, paper work, choreography, stage scenery and everything else that took most of the rest of my week to do. I did everything by myself, and after 15 years, I (and the experience) began to wear thin.

I was starting to see a different part of me, and some appropriately-timed deep insight was emerging. I discovered that just because I was doing something that I loved, didn't mean that it would totally fulfill every part of my being.

I was getting on in age—or so I certainly felt—and was starting to feel a pull to find more balance in my life; I sensed a need to pull my energies back from some of the work that I was doing with the studio.

I hoped that hiring someone to assist me would be the answer. I advertised in a local newspaper and succeeded at hiring an assistant dance teacher. What I thought was going to be a wonderful idea became a nightmare. She was late for her classes, unprepared, and would not return my phone calls. Although my students loved her, I reluctantly had to let her go. Doing this was a huge decision, since I was a quarter of the way through the dance year, had scheduled all my classes, and had split a seven-hour session with her one day each week in which she would work the first half of the evening and I the other. I had never had to fire anyone in my life, but I knew that this had to be done. I had tried many times to talk with her about the problems and I was prepared to give her one more chance; however, on a second occasion, she did not return my phone call. She was irresponsible. I wrote a letter explaining the problems again, telling her to call me. She finally did. We discussed the circumstances on the phone, and I told her that I was sorry—I had tried to be patient—but something had to change. She apologized, but I told her that things were not working out and that I would have to let her go.

There wasn't much for her to say; I think she knew that she was wrong and had over-stepped her bounds with me. I told the kids what had happened during their following classes. I said that I would take over the classes using the same songs, and everything would be all right. I felt sick to my stomach knowing that these children and their parents had no idea what was going on with this teacher behind the scenes; the kids had really enjoyed her teaching, and I wondered if their parents respected me enough to understand.

I received a call from one of my favorite student's parents that night after telling the kids the situation. She told me her daughter loved the old teacher and wasn't coming back to the dance studio anymore. I had just worked my first seven-hour session and was exhausted. I tried to explain the situation in more detail and get her to give me a chance and a little more time. I began to feel sick to my stomach and was just about to say 'hold on' when I found myself on the floor with the telephone across the room. Bob was home and came running in and I heard the mother on the other end asking if I was there. Bob picked up the phone and said hold on, as I asked him to give me a glass of orange juice. After drinking the orange juice, I began to feel better. I got back on the phone and ended the conversation saying that I would miss her daughter terribly. I was extremely over-tired, hadn't eaten, had tried to do the right thing, and never expected to lose one of my special students. The rest of the year, I worked my normal two days of dance; however, after firing the teacher, one of those days each week was a seven-hour, non-stop shift. There I was again, with no one to help me. When the year ended, I was exhausted, and I wondered if I could ever hire or trust someone to help me again.

During periods when the dance studio was closed (e.g., a few summers), I worked on Long Island in the town of Babylon doing the choreography for their musical show productions. The town provided this special program to help children who wanted to be involved in theater. Part of me felt that taking on this job was just more work, and that, during the summer, I should be concentrating on my own dance studio's September classes. Yet I always wanted to work with stage choreography, and felt that this work would both offer such experience and help me bring in some extra money.

It had been a year and a half since my experience with my dance assistant, and I was considering the idea of hiring someone else to help me again. I was in my late forties now and reluctantly feeling more tired and overwhelmed. I had always hoped that my daughter who loved to dance, would want to take over the studio. However, during this particular slice of time (which I share with you out of sequence, mirroring the non-linearity of time in our experience), Holly was married and in Potsdam with Bill, so I could not offer her the job. As I thought through my situation and pondered what I had been through before, I decided to try and find someone new to assist me, someone whom I could train slowly and someone who—eventually if things worked out—might be interested in running my dance studio, although it would continue to be in my house and I would be the owner. I had in mind that maybe during my teaching in Babylon, I would find a young dancer who would be interested in assisting me. I mentioned it to a few of my older students but they were working, going to school, or had other interests.

During my 4th summer with the town of Babylon, I was doing the choreography for the musical "Bye Bye Birdie." There were a few students whom I had taught in the past who came back for the show that year. I asked them if they were interested in assisting me with my dance studio, but after their first reaction of excitement at the idea of helping me, they too decided they could not make that kind of commitment.

There was one student whom I was teaching that year in Babylon; her name was Jennifer. She wasn't really the best dancer, but she had a loving and charming personality and a great stage presence. She not only was on-time for practices, she religiously rehearsed her dances, and was helpful to me and to the other actors in the show. Although I felt that Jennifer needed a few more years of dance technique and instruction under her belt, these deficits did not dissuade me, for I knew—this time around—that I was mainly looking for a conscientious and caring personality to assist. I wasn't ready to let go of the studio yet, and I knew that I could work with Jennifer and teach her. I decided to ask her if she was interested in helping me, and she said yes. It was vital to me, since Jennifer was only 15, to make it very clear not only to her, but to her family what I expected and what I had in mind. I invited Jennifer and her mother to my house to discuss the details. I told her and her mother the hours that she could work, what I would pay, and that—as part of the arrangement—she could take a free dance class with me. I said that I would work her slowly into assisting me, starting with helping me get the kids into their positions at the bar and lining them up to go across the floor. I told her that if she enjoyed working with me each year, I would give her more responsibility until eventually, if things worked out, I would basically give her my dance studio, allowing her the opportunity to change the name to her own and rent the space from me until she wanted to open her own storefront and get out on her own. It was an opportunity of a lifetime, and of course, they agreed with everything.

Jennifer started working for me that September, 1996. She was a genuine blessing and we got along great.

I finally was getting some long-needed relief from all of the work that I was doing alone. With each month that passed, I gave Jennifer a little more responsibility, and as months became years, she became my right arm, and special friend.

I was finally starting to let go of the dance studio a little, which allowed my Soul to emerge, and I felt like a more complete and balanced individual. I began to trust again, feeling increasingly relaxed and transformed. I was learning how to work with my inner being and was experiencing a lot less stress, as I increasingly succeeded at letting things go.

New happenings, new vibrations, new discoveries, and new people began to come into my life as a result of the extra time available in my schedule. My meditations and pensive time which originally involved me alone began to include others, and this was a very different and pleasant experience. I became knowledgeable in many new and unusual spiritual areas, most of which I had never really heard before. Much new knowledge and experience came from my time with my friend Jayne and the L.O.V.E. Center. My intuition was beginning to emerge again, and I wondered how long it had been since I had respected this side of me. The Center offered classes in Flower Reading, Guided Meditations and Breathing techniques, Past Life Regression, Dowsing, Aura Readings, Chakra System Studies, Metaphysics, Psychometry and more. The automatic writing class turned out to be an eye-opening experience.

As far back as I can remember, I enjoyed writing. When I so chose, I was able to write a poem in no time. It was easy for me, and it just seemed to flow out of my mind with beauty and grace. I knew that it was a gift, but I took it for granted, figuring it was something that anyone else in the world could do.

> *I reflect back in this moment to a day when I was a little girl. It was the summer and I was camping in the Adirondack Mountains with my family. I was spending some quiet time by myself and walking along the shore of a beautiful lake. As I pondered my surroundings, words began to flow into my mind. One word after another emerged until I mentally wrote the first of what would be many poems brought to manifestation during my lifetime. The feeling that I get in such moments of pure creation remains unparalleled.*

It wasn't until I took the automatic writing class that I realized that the beauty that came from my heart and hand might actually be involving other people or guides who were watching over me and assisting me. I hadn't worked with a guide before and didn't even really know if I had one. But I started to think more about the fact that this natural gift of mine might not be coming from just me, it might be coming from those who have always been around me, watching over me and protecting me, waiting for me to allow them to connect with me. Maybe I wasn't really alone after all, I thought?

I began to look at nature and my surroundings, taking a few moments here and there to actually appreciate the life that I was given, the health with which I had been blessed, and the person whom I was. Through books, I began to believe that I was actually a gift to the world, that my presence here meant something. The expression of God working through me grew, and I discovered the power within me of Divine presence, the power that we all hold, since we each are a part of God. I deeply understood—at a level that I had never experienced previously—the truth that I wasn't a worthless human being, and the joys in life which were always there for me to touch and hold onto; I needed only take the time to allow these joys to happen. I believed that each of us holds within us that power of perfection in all that we do, and it is our choice to recognize and use this power or not.

I was in awe at all that I was learning.

The meaning of life and why we are here was gracefully unfolding before me, and as I thought, as I asked, as I wondered all these questions, one-by-one Spirit began to reveal the answers to me. "Ask and You Shall Receive," had profound meaning to me now, and the seed, that I was, began to grow into a beautiful flower.

My life was transforming; I was happier; I wanted to share the love that I was feeling with everyone; I wanted to share the joy in my heart with the world, and I understood the truth and experienced the feeling of life and living it to its fullest.

Yes, I had accomplished many things, climbed mountains, overcome hurtles and made an amazing transformation. I felt grateful, amazed, and nurtured. I wish I could say, further, that my life was perfect and that I was in total peace. It was not, and I was not. However, I was accepting part of this gap I was feeling: I had come further than most people I knew—and was so thankful. But there were still compelling and haunting life issues that I needed to face, perhaps the greatest of all: wanting to know who my parents were. The thought of leaving this life without this information bothered me tremendously, and I prayed for answers to my questions.

The Road of Love

My Way! I yell.
I want the change Now!

Do I hear God's voice?
Do I sense God's presence?

NO!

I am so wrapped up
in what is happening in my life
I have not taken a moment to breathe
To see,
to feel His Spirit.

Why do I give my power away?

Why do I not take care of my being,
the delicate form that has been given to me?

This questioning freezes me in my tracks.

As I take the time to ponder my position,
my body,
and life's situations
I sense the signs that the Spirit World is giving me
A deep knowing and understanding envelops me

I realize ~
That life does not have to go
My Way
the way I want it,
for I do not always need to know the path,
or the outcome

I reflect back at God's care

He has always been there for me,
every step of the way

I have been able to accomplish great things,
things I never thought I could achieve
while experiencing life and
its apparent trials and tribulations

I look at this moment

I have met many challenges
and each hill has brought me new insights
New horizons
New joy and peace

At times, I could not see my way

I could not see happiness or joy
I could not see that my life's situations
could have had
very different scenarios
from the ones
that were perceived by my mind's eye

I close my eyes

I thank Spirit for my blessings,
something I have not done in a long time
I release the pressures of my life to Him
allowing Him to lead me
down the road of righteousness
the road of the unknown
The road of everlasting love

Chapter Nine

It was in the Spring of 2000 that I was preparing for a Moon Dove (women's circle) meeting. It was my turn to run the class and host the meeting. As usual, I had prepared a night fully packed with things for us to experience and do. I had completed the customary house cleaning, setting up, and prepping of water for coffee and tea. The ladies had arrived punctually, and I was soon giving my introduction when the phone rang. At first, I was upset that I had forgotten to shut the ringer off, something I routinely did before our meetings, but when I picked up the phone and heard who it was, I was extremely grateful for my mistake.

A female voice on the other end of the line asked me if my name was Christine Guardiano. I affirmed. Partially presuming another intrusive telemarketing call, I was anxious to get off the phone and get back to leading my meeting. The woman on the line said that her name was Jessica Segur.

I almost dropped the phone.

I recognized the last name immediately. It was my birth name. I continued to listen intently: body, mind, and soul all anxiously activated. The woman said that her son had received the letter I had sent and had shown it to her, because he really didn't know what to do with it. She told me that she had read the letter and saw how concerned I was to decipher my family's heath history.

The woman conjectured that she was my *aunt*—or thought she *could* be—since she was married at one time to a man named Spencer Segur, and other peculiarities may match. She continued by saying that she could possibly help me. I wanted so much to talk to her; I was so excited and wanted to spend the time asking her so many questions, but I was in the middle of my meeting, in shock, and at the time couldn't even think straight. I told her that I was presently entertaining houseguests and that I definitely wanted to speak to her more. I asked her if I could have her phone number and call her back the next day. She said yes; I thanked her, and I reluctantly hung up the phone.

A million thoughts were flying around in my head. Was this the call that I had been waiting for, or was it just someone who thought I might be a family member? Was I finally going to at-last find out about my medical history for myself and for my family? Why did this call have to come now—in the middle of my meeting? Why did I feel like I had an obligation to my friends, a responsibility to continue the meeting when this could have been the most important call of my life? Was it guilt? Was I wrong to deny myself this time and this golden opportunity? I had to trust that I was doing the right thing by getting off the phone and continuing my personal obligations. I had to trust that I had copied Jessica's number down correctly. I had to believe that this was all happening the way it was for some divinely bizarre reason. My heart was beating fast. I wanted to cry from joy and excitement. I wanted this special moment to be the moment I had been waiting for.

I walked back into my living room with a look of, I guess, shock on my face. "Are you all right?" was ringing from (seemingly) disembodied voices and from concerned, loving faces from around the room. I paused for only the slightest moment and then told the women what had just happened. The room exploded in a symphony of joyous animation and excitement. These women all had known how long I had been praying and hoping for some kind of response or answer to my prayers and to my letters, and now it looked like my dreams may have come true. But why had I hung up the phone, they asked? I can't even remember the lame answer I gave to their question; I continued on with the meeting. The rest of the evening and night dragged on for me. The women said good-bye, each one making me promise that I would call her as soon as I had spoken again to the mystery-filled woman.

I could hardly sleep, waiting for morning and the chance to call Jessica back. It had to be one of the longest nights in my life. Question after question swam through my mind. I wanted Jessica to be part of my family, but was she? I tried not to get my hopes up, afraid that I might come to another dead-end, but there was no suppressing my hope.

On the first try the next morning, I was able to connect directly with Jessica. Her voice was steady and neutral. To me, it was hard to tell how old she was, but she sounded maybe between 60 and 70 years old. The expression in her voice was of concern and compassion for what I was going through. This sudden entrant into my life started to tell me a whirlwind story of why she felt that I could be her niece. I was overwhelmed with what I was hearing, and I was trying to write down, as fast as I could, everything that she was saying in some kind of sensible order.

The woman told me that her deceased husband had been one of four siblings, the only male. The oldest sibling in the Segur family was Mabel, followed by Esther, Madelyn, and Spencer. Spencer was Jessica's husband. All of the siblings were now dead, Jessica said, except Mabel. Jessica wasn't sure what she thought the family would really want me to know, but she continued.

It seemed that depression ran in this family. Spencer had taken his own life. He had done it in front of Jessica by sticking a gun in his mouth and blowing his head off, leaving her in psychological shock, with a young son to raise on her own.

Esther passed away following freak complications from a flu shot. Evidentially, she didn't know that she had a case of lobar pneumonia at the time of her injection. Within 5 hours of receiving the flu shot, Esther Segur was dead.

Madelyn, who appears *not* to have been the most respected member of the family, was a gadabout. It was commonly reported that she had been with one guy after another and had given birth to several children. The first two seemingly were "taken from" her by authorities. Jessica didn't say, but I assumed it must have had something to do with Madelyn being judged as some kind of unfit mother. Another child was reportedly adopted, formally or informally, by extended family somewhere distant. A fourth child also existed, Jessica said. It was this fourth child that may well have been the reason for us two strangers talking decades later. Jessica said that *I* very well *might be* that fourth child of Madelyn's.

A thunderous cacophony of thoughts and feelings swirled in a four-dimensional rollercoaster inside my being.

In the years that *I* had been moving rapidly into adulthood—progressing through all of the challenges and triumphs I've so far described to you in this book—a group of people a universe away, in a seemingly unrelated world, apparently were observing a woman named Madelyn becoming increasingly depressed; this one of four Segur siblings was noticeably distraught.

Jessica went on to say that one day in April 1975, while living in Florida near Jessica, Madelyn—possibly my natural birth mother—died from an overdose of liquor and drugs. The death certificate records her passing as a suicide. Jessica told me, however, that she and others have long questioned her sister-in-law's death. Madelyn had been in a visibly troubled personal relationship at the time, and speculation in the community suggested that maybe Madelyn was *murdered.*

Mabel was the only one of her deceased husband's siblings still *alive,* Jessica said. Since the death of her husband, Jessica has spoken to Mabel only on a rare occasion. Jessica herself could not confirm that I was definitely a family member, but she told me that, since Mabel was the closest living testament to what happened, she would contact her only remaining sister-in-law and ask her for her information.

Before hanging up the phone with Jessica, I told this important new person in my life that it might be helpful if I sent her some of our family pictures to see if she could detect any physical resemblance of our families. Jessica indicated that sending such photos would be a wonderful idea, and I told her that I would gather and

155 - Christine Guardiano

mail them in the next few days. In the meantime, she said that she would speak to Mabel and get back to me with any information she could find.

That night, I went through all my pictures, labeled them, and organized the ones that I wanted to send. There were pictures of myself, Holly, Nick, my brother, and of course my husband Bob at all different stages of our lives. Bob mailed them out for me the next morning. I was anxious to hear back from Jessica and see what she thought.

I relayed this incredible update to all of my friends-in-waiting, and they were all praying for me. In our own home, Nick and Bob didn't have much of a reaction, but Holly was as excited as I was. I know that she too wanted to know more family history, especially concerning the cancer.

[Part of my Holly/health-oriented search involved looking into the background of my *husband's* family. Bob's mother had passed away when he was 11 years old, and he too did not know much about her or her family. His father and new stepmother took care of Bob and his sister as they grew, so Bob had some insight into his dad's side of the family, but not much information on his mother's. The information about Bob's family was just as important to me, since part of my search was to try and find out if Holly's cancer was hereditary. I was able to contact a family member who gave us some family history. He said there was no cancer in the family that he knew of. I followed my intuition and let that be.]

It was no more than a week after we shipped the photos that, upon arrival home from running some errands, I was greeted by the gently flashing light of our answering machine. I put my things away and then went to listen to the message. "Christine!" I heard. It was Jessica's voice. "Oh my God you are definitely a Segur!" she continued. "I received your pictures, and you look *a lot* like Madelyn, and *your daughter* Holly does even more. She looks just like her. I can see it in her eyes!"

I couldn't believe what I was hearing. I started to cry. I played the tape again to confirm that I wasn't dreaming.

I called Jessica back right away. She was so excited. She couldn't believe the family resemblance. Of course I had to take her word for it, since I myself had no reason to doubt her. However, I wanted to see it for myself. At that point, Jessica had not spoken to Mabel. Jessica told me that she would send Mabel the pictures and then have Mabel send them back to me once Mabel—the only living Segur sibling—had a chance to look at them.

Another week went by and nothing. I had asked Jessica if maybe she could look for some pictures so I could see for myself the uncanny resemblance that she was talking about. Two weeks later, an envelope came in the mail. Enclosed was a letter from Mabel, along with the photos I had sent them and some pictures of the Segur family. This is what the letter said:

Christine:

 I have enclosed some copies of photos of my sister and my brother. I am sure you will see what I see. These snapshots are quite old and did not copy well.

 Christine, I must tell you that you are better off with being raised by responsible parents who loved you and still do. I do not have to meet your family to know that. You have no idea where or how you would have lived had my sister not put you up for adoption. I know this must hurt and I am sorry to be the one to tell you this; however, she just walked away from responsibility and never looked back. She had a loving family and was not raised any differently than her siblings. Who knows why some family members turn out one way and others another way altogether. Nothing can change the past, and perhaps it is better to leave well enough alone. I can understand your wanting to know all you can about your biological mother. There is nothing to say, except that she came from good people, who were clean, law-abiding citizens who were hard workers that loved and took care of their families. Why she turned out differently, we will never know.

Love always, Mabel

I knew that what Mabel had written was true. Her letter touched my heart. I began to look at the pictures one by one, studying each one in detail. The first one was a picture of Jessica, Spencer, and their son. The second was a picture of Esther in a dance costume—how strangely poignant. I saw myself in her: the eyes the expression, especially the second picture of her when she was older.

Then there was the picture of Madelyn, my possible—even probable?!—birth mother.

I could see what Jessica and Mabel were talking about. Madelyn did remind me of my daughter. And yes—there was something in the eyes. The last was a shot of Mabel. How beautiful she was. My heart went out to her and the life that she had been through. How much she wanted a normal family, but for her, it was not meant to be. I prayed that she had found some happiness amidst all of the death and destruction.

My feelings were all over the place. I wanted to meet Mabel and talk to her. I had so many questions. However, I did not want to disrupt her life. I knew that Jessica could not tell me much about my possible birth mom. I knew one thing and that was: I certainly was lucky to have grown up in a loving family. I realized how different my life would have been if this were not so. I knew deep down that many of the positive things that I had experienced and gone through would never have occurred if my life had been different in the way that I sometimes had dreamed, as a child. I know how sensitive I was and how depressed I had been in the past.

A great knowing came over me that this was the life I was supposed to live, where and who I was supposed to be.

I wondered if I would have been half the person I am now, if I had grown up in a Segur household. Would I have had the courage to go to college, leave my first husband, or start my own dance studio? It was then, as I looked at Mabel's letter and at the pictures from that other world, that I knew that <u>this</u> was the place and plan that was set for me and my life so long ago. I was not supposed to be a Segur, I was supposed to be Christine, not Kathy, and find the strength <u>within</u> me to change my life and touch the lives of so many people in many different ways. And although this truth and revelation brought me unprecedented comfort and joy, I hoped that some day, I could meet the last Segur family member that

I knew or find a way to be 100% sure that this was my birth-family.

I wrote Mabel and asked her about the Segur family history, since this was of utmost importance to me. I also asked her if we could meet. A few weeks went by and I got another letter. This time it arrived via the Internet. She said that as far as she knew, there was no cancer found in the family. There had been depression and heart disease. The knowledge of this gave me some relief, but how much family history was there really since so many members had died young?

Mabel skirted the issue of us getting together.

She said that she did a lot of traveling and would see what would happen in the future. When I mentioned to Jessica that I wanted to meet Mabel and that she did a lot of traveling, Jessica said that maybe part of the reason Mabel was avoiding a meeting was because of her husband. She said that he knew everything that Mabel had gone through in her life and probably was protecting her from bringing up past memories that might upset her. I understood this, and decided to wait for a while before I reached out again.

I thought about having Mabel do a DNA test, but I was afraid to ask her. I was not sure if she would approve. Yet did any of this really matter anymore? Why did I always have to question and wonder?

I thought I would present the pictures and letter to my adopted mom (my real mom). My main reason for doing so was to set her mind at ease. I knew deep down that she was worried about what I would find out or how my feelings for her might change. I hoped that if I shared the information that I had found and the letter from Mabel that mom's mind might be put at ease. I made a lunch date with my mother; she agreed to it.

I was a little nervous, but kept a positive perspective as Mom and I sat at the table, mother and daughter. We ordered our meals, and while we were waiting for them to come, I told my mom that I had most likely found my birth family. Her eyes widened, I think she was a little afraid of what I was going to say. I continued by telling her that there were four children in the family and three were dead. One family member named Mabel was the only one that I knew who was alive and she had sent me some pictures and a letter that I wanted her to read. I took the letter and pictures from my purse and handed them to the woman who had raised me. I was not sure what her reaction would be.

She looked at the pictures as I explained who each family member was; she said that she saw no family resemblance.

This did not surprise me. Then she picked up the letter and for a minute or two she read it intently and then looked up at me and said that Mabel was right. I knew what she meant. My family had loved me and taken care of me, and I was certainly a lot better off where I was. I told my mom that I had always loved her and appreciated her taking care of me and giving me a home. I told her that she was my mother and always would be. Although I had told her this same thing a thousand times before, this time there was a change in her expression, a sigh of relief, a final moment of internal peace. She did not have to say anything to me; she expressed it all with her eyes. Her eyes that had loved me all my life, but were afraid to express her deepest feelings and fears. In that moment, time stood still and the weight of the world that had so heavily laid over our relationship disappeared, and joy was born.

Our relationship made a complete turnaround that day. There was a new respect for each other and who we were. My mom began to treat me as an adult and not just her child. We spoke more freely about things and began to confide more in each other, sharing our deepest feelings, those that had never been expressed out of fear, the fear that came from me of always worrying about what my mother might say; and her fear of always having to be the adult and not feeling comfortable enough to show her soft side. To this day, I am not sure of all the changes that took place, but for the first time in my life, I had the mom I always dreamed about. Even Bob noticed the change between us.

I had finally found the connection, closeness, and respect that I felt had been missing all my life.

~

I noticed that although things with my mom and me were often strained, mom's relationship with my brother was very different. I would get nervous whenever I did anything wrong, yet Gordon would have the strength that I didn't have to fight back. I think somehow my mom knew that Gordon was his own person and she could not control him very easily. With me, she knew my weaknesses and lack of confidence and played upon these conditions to occasionally try and control me. Gordon, as I have said, had his moments of getting into trouble as he was growing up, and my mother and father would often have a run in with him when he would misbehave. My parents would yell at him, ground him, or hit him with the strap if he was really bad. I loved him so much and hated it when he was punished, so I dared not tell on him. The standard joke between my brother and me was that if we started to tell my parents all of the things that we had done wrong, we would be telling them stories from now until doomsday.

So many things that my brother did, I kept secret, and would not tell my parents. Somehow, though, my mom always seemed to find things out eventually, like the time that she thought my brother was dressed all nicely for school, and our neighbor Mrs. Spira, found clothes tucked under the bush in her yard. These were the ones my mom thought Gordon was wearing; however, he had his tight jeans (that I would take in for him on the sewing machine) and his black leather jacket hidden in his bag. He wanted to look like a hood, not a nerd. Then there was the time that he and his friends asked me for a pair of scissors when my mom was at work. I lent them out, only to find the boys returned to the door a few minutes later holding not just the scissors but also the small intestines of some roadkill hanging from each blade. The boys had thought it amusing to perform a complete dissection on the side of the road. I almost threw up! Gordon was into everything, no holds barred. My mom didn't know what to do because he always was into something.

One day, a neighbor came to the house asking mom if she had a son around 12 years old. My mom, who had endured enough of my brother's shenanigans, said "no", even though Gordon was 11. My poor mom that day just couldn't face *another* of Gordon's misbehaviors, so she felt that if the lady didn't guess his age right, one could legitimately tell this woman that my mom had no such son 'around' the age of *twelve*.

I hated it when my brother got into trouble. I cried when he was spanked. However, there were a few times I would tell on my brother, especially if it was something I felt was dangerous, like the time he cut a hole in the wood floor of his bedroom to hide fireworks. My father made him put the fireworks in water to destroy them. I felt terrible because I knew that my brother had spent a lot of money on them but, I could not stand the thought that he might get badly hurt if I did not tell on him.

Yes, my brother and I had our moments, which also included hiding under the stairs together and grabbing the babysitter's leg as she descended, looking for us. No wonder she never sat for us anymore. Or the time we took the leaf bags from the neighborhood and dragged them down the street from the car until they broke, sending leaves spiraling and whirling all over the neighbors' yards.

I enjoyed spending time with my brother, and I have many wonderful memories with him: camping and hiking through the forest, going to the park to swing on the swing, and hanging out in his room. It didn't matter. I always looked forward to being able to share those special moments and am grateful to this day for the wonderful memories that those times with my brother made for me.

Family closeness and relationships have always been important to me. I know that I didn't feel very free to share my feelings with my parents, but I wanted *my children* to feel free enough to come to me at any time. I certainly did not expect them to tell me everything, but I did want them to be *unafraid* to ask for help if they needed it. Holly and I never had a problem sharing our feelings as she grew up. We would have our fights, which she thought were quite funny, since she always seemed to be quicker than me and have the last word. However with my son and myself, it was different. Nick had problems speaking when he was little and I am not sure if it had anything to do with those troubles, but, growing up, he didn't have much to say. When Nick did express himself, I found him to be very negative, and I would worry that he might be very depressed. I tried to reach him a few times, but found it difficult. His typical response to me would be one word or a grunt. It wasn't until Nick finished high school and went away from home that our seeming communication barrier dissolved. Since that time, Nick has shone expressively as a very respectful, talkative, loving, and caring person. As I write this, I couldn't be more proud of him or grateful for our relationship and *all* of its phases of evolution.

I have often encountered people having trouble communicating with their children. I know that I pushed too hard at times with my son Nick. I can remember yelling and fighting with him, which got neither of us anywhere. I finally saw a change in him when I let go, stopped forcing my feelings upon him, expressed my inner feelings, and did it all from love. It is not easy to do this, for we tend to get wrapped up in the situation and what is happening, and we can not see clearly how to solve the problems we go through from a loving point of view. When we take the time to focus and express ourselves with love in our hearts, miracles happen.

As a child, Nick had been, one might say "a handful." My mom would say that I ended up with the same kind of children that she had and said that my troubles with Nick were partly a blessing in that they would help me totally understand what she went through. Nick was a colicky baby, and as I said earlier, he had problems with his ears and speech. He was a frustrated child, for we often could not understand what he was trying to say, and he would act out to get our attention and make his point: he would hide under the table when the babysitter would come, throw himself on the floor in the shopping malls, and even use the clothes pole in his closet to ramrod the door when we locked him in his room to discipline him. Nick was a very active child, always on the go. Although I was often concerned about him since he didn't share his feelings, I knew that he was basically happy: I often saw him smile. He loved camping, playing family games, wrestling with his dad, and playing with his sister (whenever Holly had the patience for him). He played soccer, baseball, hockey, skateboarding and biking. And of course, there were the normal mishaps as he burned his neck, his wrist, his hand; and cut open his eyelid, his chin, and his head.

There was always something going on in Nick's life, and I was happy that he had many friends. I hoped that he could at least share his personal feelings with them, since communication at home was sometimes difficult. I think that maybe the reason my son became less talkative in his teens was because he found most conversation pointless or of no interest to him. This reality/perception, of course, just led to different kinds of problems between us, since I wanted so much to find some way of communicating with him. When Nick was around 16 or 17, I became concerned with his lack of communication and wrote him a series of letters, telling him how I felt. I had tried to have a few heart-to-heart talks with my son, but we were just not making a connection. Eventually, through the letters, my verbal concern and love, and Nick's increased receptivity, there was a gradual break-through in our relationship. Communication flowed and a renewed respect and understanding for each other came. Nick developed a real love for school once he was in college, and my son became an independent young man. It really wasn't until this point in his life that I finally got to know my son, my son who rarely shared his feelings. Maybe it was because he was finally really happy to be alive and was finding life worth living now that he encountered something that interested him in college. I don't know, but as I spoke to him, I finally saw his love for life, his compassion for others, and his love for me.

The beauty was in the little things that my son said and did: the effort that he would take in finding the perfect gift at Christmas; asking me and others if we were all right; helping his friends in need; working hard and being respectful on his jobs; and laughing and sharing his life with his family—all things he never did before. I know that Nick's younger years were not easy for him, and like I said, it wasn't an easy road. He has accomplished much in his life and continues to strive and to achieve his dreams and goals. I am proud of the things that he has accomplished and the compassionate man he has become.

~

So it seemed that I was coming to a new road in my life. My son and I were enjoying a new richness in our relationship. I had been through the worst with a daughter who faced cancer, and now she seemed to be on the road to recovery. My life was changing spiritually, and I was beginning to find inner peace. I was grateful for the time to regroup and go on with a more mundane life for a while.

Sometimes my mind would drift back casually through time gone by...

Holly and Bill were living on their own here on Long Island, but were having personal problems. I think my daughter hoped that things would smooth out between the two of them. On the rare occasion when she would say something to me about the situation, I listened but didn't worry or give it much thought. I felt for sure that within time all would be well. After all, my daughter and her groom had married young, lived on their own, owned a business, closed a business, moved into our home, gone through a cancer scare and moved back out on their own, all in 2 years. We were certain that whatever they were going through at this point in their lives, strength and love would prevail.

However, even if strength and love prevailed (in perhaps a most obtuse way), the marriage of Holly and Bill did not endure.

It was the fall of 1999 when Holly and Bill went upstate to Potsdam to visit Bill's parents. During this trip, Holly had a spiritual revelation. She was on a hike with Bill and his family, and since it hadn't been that long after her operation, Holly found herself growing very tired as she climbed the mountain. Bill wanted her to reach the top to see the beautiful sunset, but she told him and his family that she would be fine by herself and invited them to go on without her. She sat down by herself to rest and began to look around the forest. It was so beautiful in the sunlight as the sun's rays streamed through the trees. On the ground were many beautiful colored leaves and she began to pick them up one by one. How beautiful each one was individually, each with its own color, shape, and size. As my daughter continued this process, a tremendous peace came over her, and she realized how beautiful and precious life was. Each living thing that surrounded her had its own importance and place in the universal scheme of things, including herself, and she knew then—at that moment—the magnificence and love of the Divine.

From the experience of this simple hike through the woods, a new outlook on life began. Holly had begun her own spiritual journey of empowerment and peace. She started to look at life situations and to view them in a different light, especially the one dealing with her husband Bill.

About a year after her connection with those colorful leaves—and perhaps her connection with something far deeper—Holly told us that she and her husband were separating.

We were surprised. My daughter told us that she still loved her husband with all of her heart, but she saw now that their goals, life interests, religious beliefs, and ideas about children were very different. Efforts had been made to overcome these differences, but the chasm proved to be increasing, not diminishing. Bill did not want to accompany Holly for couples' counseling, but Holly felt there was a need. Although the separation was killing her inside, Holly knew that she and Bill were very different. It was a blessing that they had no children, and she felt that they would be happier, each starting a new life alone. Holly was willing to give up her relationship with Bill, even though she still loved him, because she felt that they each could find more happiness with someone else—with partners who would have the same ideas and goals as they each did, respectively. I was surprised at the change of heart that seemed—to Bob and me—to come almost out of the blue. Where did this originate, I wondered? Did it have anything to do with what Holly had been through? The answers to my questions would [eventually] be forthcoming.

I shared all the interesting news about the Segur family with Holly the following spring, as I learned each new piece of information. My daughter was shocked to hear both about my tremendous breakthrough and about how tragic life was for the family. There seemed to be a sense of great understanding that came from within my daughter when I told her about my mother, her life, her depression, and the different relationships with men. I felt that Holly somehow knew exactly what Madelyn had gone through. We mulled over the facts together, trying to figure out in our minds what might have happened in Madelyn's life that led her to her death. Madelyn had been born on January 30th, 1927 and had killed herself in April of 1975. She was only forty-eight when she passed away. Truly still a young woman with much life ahead of her. Why would she kill herself? Had she gone to Heaven? After all, if she wasn't murdered, it certainly was not God's time. She had chosen to end her life. This process of searching for answers to these questions continued in Holly's mind and my own mind even when we were not together.

I had read a variety of things on suicide and had heard many things. Some people believed that you went to Hell if you took your own life. Some felt that you were taken care of by the angels until you again felt loved and healed. Others thought that if the life had been terminated and there were still lessons that needed to be learned, you would return in another's body to finish that process.

I certainly did not believe in Hell. The thought of the angels caring for you was beautiful, and as far as coming back in another form to finish your life, I didn't know. I hadn't read much on that subject, but I certainly was open-minded about it.

One day, when I was thinking through all of the aforementioned scenarios, an emotional thought came into my mind. These were the facts. Madelyn died in April 1975; Holly was conceived in April 1975. Madelyn had been born January 30, and although my due date with Holly was set for February, she was born on January 29th, at 11:07PM, less than an hour before January 30th. Just coincidence?

Due to toxemia, I had been put into the hospital early. The doctor induced labor but nothing was happening. At around 10:30PM he came into the room and told me he felt there was no way the baby was going to be born before midnight. I couldn't believe what he was telling me. I was feeling so much pressure. But what did I know? This was my first child. I just could not see how this was going to take over another hour, and I was holding back from pushing. I didn't want to push too early, for I was afraid my vagina would rip. I was grateful that my husband was there, and at about 10:50PM I asked him to get the nurse. When she came into the room, she took one look at me and called the doctor. Before I knew what was happening, they were wheeling me into the delivery room, telling me that I had to start pushing, for I was slowing down the baby's heartbeat. They said that if the baby were not born soon, I would have to have a C-section. I did not need to hear more. Holly was born almost instantaneously after that.

I found it very unusual the way that all of the facts fell into place. This brought more questions to mind. Could it be that because Madelyn had killed herself and left behind unfinished business, that she had returned in the body of my daughter to be born almost on her own birthday? The idea was bizarre but _very_ interesting.

I wished that I could think of some way to know for certain that Madelyn was my birth mother. I felt happy that I was getting some supposed answers, but there was no solid proof. I was frustrated, yet there was nothing that I could do. I felt as if life were teasing me, placing me back at Square One, to wonder for the rest of my life what the real truth was. How unfair could things be?

It was time again for Holly to go for another CAT scan. This was her second one. Every time she went in, we would hold our breath waiting for the results.

This time, the results were not very good: the doctors had found another cyst on her existing ovary. This one was much smaller than the last, so the doctor told her to come back in three months and have a sonogram to keep on top of it. I couldn't believe it. Hadn't my daughter been through enough? How much more was my little girl supposed to handle?

Holly seemed to take the information well. She told me that she wasn't overly concerned, since she did not have any pain, and she would know if the problem was getting out-of-hand because of what she had gone through before. I was happy that this cyst had been found early and was glad that the doctors were going to keep on top of it. I hoped that Holly would do the same. After all, when she had the cancer the first time and the cyst was so big, she also didn't have any pain.

Sometimes I felt that Life was handing me more than I could handle. My spirituality had helped me grow stronger and see things more clearly. Yet there were still times that I felt like I was drowning. I asked myself what was holding me back from creating the peaceful life that I believed I could make for myself? Was there something that I could do to fix my emotional state? There I went again off on a tangent of trying to control my situation. After all, I had so many blessings in my life. Why wasn't I appreciating them more? I knew that life held good and bad, challenges and miracles. Were these opposites placed before me to balance my perspectives and help me become more aware of the beauty in my world?

A very special person Rev. Dr. Janine Burns said once that "Shift Happens." She explained how we go through our life saying "Why Me?" and "Shit Happens," whenever something goes wrong. Maybe we should stop and look at life in another way? Realize that things that are happening to us are for a positive reason to move us forward from one point of our lives to another. If "Shit" didn't "Happen," maybe we would not move from one place to the other, and we would stay stagnant for long periods of time. Should we look at the "Shit" as a "Shift" instead? Could this be a possible way for God to work through and with us? Could it be a means of getting us to that special place, which we otherwise might not have reached? A shifting from one state of being to the next often forces us to make changes in our lives through challenges and through trial-and-error. Maybe we are not meant to control our lives' outcomes? Maybe we should be more accepting of our circumstances and more trusting of our future?

I listened and heard all of this, but it did not sink in. I wanted it my way. Not God's way.

Little Warrior

From morning to night,
all is the same
We awaken and realize
there has been no change

Our life is revolving;
no newness is found:
The boredom, depression,
of things cycling around

Are we too afraid
to step out of our box?
That unfamiliar feeling
has our stomachs tied in knots.

The fear of the unknown,
the questions in our mind
bring us down in the dumps
and our Spirit they do bind

We must allow the shift to happen
permit the changes to take place,
Be brave enough to challenge
all of the burdens on our plate

Be strong enough
to emerge from the darkness
into the light
Where joy, peace, and new beginnings
bring each one of us insights

Yes ~
the first step can be difficult;
we must let go, trust, and believe;
then, a new life will surround us
and happiness we will receive.
For life wants us to move forward;
we are here to learn and be alive
For the Spirit which lies within us
Needs to grow and be revived

So allow for new beginnings!
Open up to each new day!
Enjoy the journey and excitement...
Let your soul be born today!
Let your heart guide each new morning
with positive energy and thoughts
Let each new day shine upon you,
and you never will feel lost.

Chapter Ten

In summer 1999, **shift** was happening in many aspects of my life. I was in my late forties at this time and feeling more tired and drained. The dance studio, which had been a dream come-true, was beginning to overwhelm me. Although I had the 19 year-old Miss Jen assisting me, I longed for more peace and space. I was being drawn to examine the true meaning of why I was here on Earth and what was really important in life. The dance studio had fulfilled me in many ways, but I was undeniably also being led to work more on my own spiritual growth.

Even amidst these strong feelings of personal spiritual (r)evolution, I loved the studio and did not want to give it up. It was my life, my joy, and most of all: the studio is who I was. It was the physical and metaphysical place where I routinely found myself, where I received love, and it was one of my few sources of happiness. Yet part of me was beginning to urge a letting go of the studio. Another part of me held to it with the same vigor that a child steadfastly holds onto a favorite blanket for safety. I felt nurtured by and attached to the studio. I also felt it was my choice to decide when my transition out of the studio would happen. All I had to do was open my mouth and ask Miss Jen if she felt ready to run the dance studio on her own. I was pretty sure that she would say 'yes,' since she had been learning and working with me during the past 3 years.

I felt great conflict each day as the energy of my status vis-à-vis the studio began consuming me.   I felt that if I let go of the dance studio, I would be losing a part of myself, part of who I was. I had gained so much from it over the past *twelve* years, and it was my baby. I had given birth to it with all the strength that was inside of me, and now Spirit was asking me to examine my connection to it and how important it really was.

Although I knew most deeply within, that now it was time to let go, time to retire, and time to move on, I couldn't bring myself to speak the words to Miss Jen. I think part of me wanted some kind of security net to fall into. I was having trouble imagining what I was going to do—and who I was going to be—without the studio as part of my life, since it had become an all-consuming job, taking up most of my time. Over and over, thoughts raced through my head, until one day Spirit, in no uncertain terms, made it perfectly clear:

I was in the middle of doing laundry, and had just pulled the clothes out of the dryer, folded them, and placed them in the laundry basket for hauling upstairs to the bedrooms. My mind had clattered ceaselessly throughout. As I walked out of the laundry room, I heard a voice out of the blue and as clear as a bell say to me "Will you cut the shit!!!" I was in shock. I almost turned around to see who was there when I realized that it was Spirit talking to me. What I found most amusing was the way the message was delivered. The words were perfect, got my attention, and made me think. It wasn't until that point that I realized how much I had been driving myself nuts, thinking my problem over and over to death. I knew then that it was time for me to make the move no matter how difficult it might be.

I spoke to Miss Jen and told her that in September 1999, she could run the dance studio, unless, of course, she wanted me to help her one more year. Was it that I didn't want her to feel overwhelmed by taking over the studio right away, or was I trying to hold on for one more year?

I don't know, but the decision was made for me, when Miss Jen told me that she was ready to take over the studio.

Everything had fallen into place just the way it was supposed to. It was me who was fighting my intuition, the obvious, and the direction in which Spirit was trying to lead me. I was the one who was blind to the signs, the one who didn't want to see them. Sure I wanted a more peaceful life, but I wasn't willing to look at the subtle hints that Spirit was trying to give me. Again there was the issue of control: the control that I have fought with most of my life. I wanted to be the one who said when, where, how, and why. Giving myself over to a higher power's guidance was not yet a part of who I was.

How many times do signs show up in our lives that we just ignore? God has given us our five senses and we do not use them to their potential. Sure we can see, taste, smell, touch and feel, but can we use these senses beyond our immediate reality? It is my experience that signs are given to us every day—in everyday language, not requiring extrasensory perception to decode. It is just a matter of whether we choose to experience and recognize these signs or not.

Miss Jen was excited about taking over the studio, and in explaining some of the groundwork, I told her that I would be there to help her in any way that I could. I told her that she would need her own insurance policy and that it would be nice for her to register her own studio name so she could start a DBA ("doing business as") checking and savings account.

During the next few months, we threw around different names for the studio. It had been my experience that it was helpful to have more than one name chosen in case the name was already taken by another company.

I was in my car with my husband Bob one day when I noticed an interesting license plate on the car in front of us. Looking at license plates of cars was not something I usually did. The license plate said "Next Step." I couldn't believe what I was reading. Was I being given a sign? I looked at my husband and said that it would be the perfect name for Miss Jen's dance studio. My husband—being the practical man—said that it was a great name, but that I shouldn't force it on Miss Jen. I told him I would never do that, but that I had to tell her. As it turned out, Miss Jen loved the name as much as I did. It was perfect. Her studio was the next step and of course it was the perfect name for a dance studio. We gathered that name and others together and went to the town clerk's office to register her name. We gave the person behind the desk the name "Next Step" and she said it was fine. I looked at Jen and she looked at me. We both could not believe that it was so easy. At that point it was very obvious to both of us that this was what her studio was supposed to be called.

June 1999 came to an end and my last recital was a tear-jerker as I hugged each child who I had taught over the past year. The families went home saying their good-byes and thanking me for all that I had done and all the love that I had extended to their children. We cleared the stage from the show and sent our summer wishes to all who had lent a hand.

I was finally alone for a moment. I turned and walked out onto the darkened stage. As I gazed out into the empty chairs that an audience usually occupied, I thanked Spirit for everything it had given me. The strength that I had obtained, the woman who I had become, the courage, the beauty, the friends and most importantly, the confidence that I so greatly needed within myself. I knew that although I was leaving this part of my life behind, great growth had occurred in me. One last tear fell from my eye; I took a deep breath, and walked off the stage for the last time as a dance studio director.

Giving up the studio was one of the hardest things I have ever had to do in my life, and I think my daughter knew it. She, with the help of my husband, had planned a surprise retirement party for me in my own backyard a few weeks after the recital. All of the kids were there with their families to wish me well and to again thank me for teaching them. Although I was pleased with all the love and effort that went into planning the party, I found it difficult to spend time with all of these people again. It wasn't that I was unsure of my decision; it's just that deep down inside I was still hurting, and I wanted to make that clean break and move on. I wasn't able to eat and really enjoy the party the way I had hoped to, and when I saw the book that my daughter had worked hard to make for me of all the pictures of the past dance recitals, I started crying all over again.

I still had questions in my mind of how I was going to cope with the dance studio that was still going to be running out of my home. How I was going to see the kids whom I had taught week after week and not be involved. I knew that I had to do something to occupy my time and energy.

My wish came true when I went to a concert at a church in Huntington Station called the "New Thought Spiritual Center." I had made reservations over the phone with a woman named Janine, but was not familiar with the voice. When I walked into the concert, she was there greeting everyone and recognized me right away. We had known each other from growing up in the same Lutheran church in Huntington and hadn't seen each other in at least 35 years. I was surprised to see her and was also amazed that she even knew me. During the evening, we got talking about how she was so overwhelmed with running the church and was thinking of moving out on her own as a private minister. I was empathetic to her needs, for I understood everything she was going through. I told her that I too had felt a calling to move on with my life and had just given up the dance studio that I had been running for years. She asked me if I could help her out now and then with some paperwork in order to take the burden off of her a little. I was happy to do it once or twice a week, which I did for the next six months to a year until Rev. Janine was ready to move into her private practice. During that time, although it was a lot of work, we had much fun and my power of positive thinking was reinforced by this woman. I read Ernest Homes' book and learned much about positive thought and manifestation. It was an unexplainably valuable experience for me, and I learned a lot from Janine. We each became an angel to the other as we helped, strengthened, and supported each other in a time of mutual need. Most of all, this experience kept my mind busy and away from thinking so much about the dance studio.

September came and Miss Jen was raring to go with the start of her studio. Most of the kids were fine with the change since she had been working with me for the past three years. I had told her it would be a lot of work, and she found this to be true, but her love of the studio—like mine—kept her moving forward to the completion of the year.

Myself, I did well. There were a couple of twinges in my heart as I heard the voice of some of my former students echoing down the halls of my home. Yet I kept firm to what I had told Miss Jen: I felt it was best for me to stay clear of what was going on as much as possible. However, I let Miss Jen know that she could come upstairs to ask me questions at any time. On occasion she needed my help, but for the most part she did a wonderful job directing and teaching her students.

And so, at age 48 I began a new stage of my life. The pressure was off, and as time went on, I felt a great relief. Doing the yard- and housework became less stressful too, and I felt—for the first time in many years—peaceful. I began to find more time to meditate and read. My intuition was growing and was beginning to develop. During meditation, I started to see signs, receiving messages from Spirit and finding their meaning in books that I had collected. I even began to see auras and what I call nature's grid. This was the geometric makeup of objects—such as air, rock, and other interesting things—that I had never seen before.

One of the most profound moments came one evening when I was sitting quietly in a group with other people sitting around me, listening to their conversations. My eyes fell upon one person who was on the ground to the right of me. As I looked at the person and smiled, I noticed that this person was sitting in golden dust that was like a small cloud hovering around the person's body. I felt an enormous sense of peace, comfort, protection and love come over me. This feeling was so strong that I remember thinking to myself that a bomb could drop and it wouldn't matter. I knew I was safe and protected even under the most horrendous of circumstances. This feeling was so strong, that I wanted to cry from the sheer overwhelming sense of unconditional love. I wasn't that sure at the time what had happened, but from talking to others about the experience and reading about it, I believe that for a moment I was able to make a soul connection with this beautiful human being. After all, one person said to me "Aren't the eyes the window of the soul?" To this day I don't know why this incident happened, but I felt for a moment that I had touched heaven on earth. I had hoped that I would experience this again in my life, but to this day I have not. It would be wonderful if it did happen again, yet maybe once was enough to let me know God's love is there even when we least expect it.

~

Holly continued ignoring the cyst that was on her ovary. I was not at all happy about this. It was time again for her to go for another CAT scan. It had already been over a year since her last exam, and I told her that I was worried. She said she knew she was fine and that she would go for another test soon. This was my daughter and I couldn't do much about it. I just kept praying that she would be fine.

At the time, Holly had decided to separate from Bill and she was in the process of looking for her own place that she could afford on her own. I did understand the stress she was under, so I tried not to push too hard with her health. She was able to find a nice one-bedroom apartment in the town of Huntington and Bob, Bill, Holly and I all helped move her in. Bill went on his way and moved in with a friend. Although Holly and Bill were no longer living together, they did stay in touch and remained friends. Bob and I would see Bill on occasion when he would stop by for his mail, and since we did still love him, it was nice to be able to stay in touch this way. Of course this would not have been the case if Holly did not approve. But she knew Bill had no family on Long Island and felt comfortable about his visits.

Holly and I were talking about the Segur family and both of us wanted to meet them. Mabel seemed very reluctant, but Jessica—in Florida—was hoping we would come down for a visit. Without mentioning the trip to my mom, in fear of what she would say or how she would worry, we worked out a time and day that would be good for the Segur family and for Holly and me. The two of us, mother and daughter, flew down to Florida not only to meet this part of the Segur family but also to have a little vacation time. We both had been through a lot. We planned some time in Disney World and then a few days to meet Jessica and her new husband Ernie

Once in Florida we rented a convertible and set off to Disney. It was wonderful seeing all the beautiful places, having downtime and one-on-one space with my daughter. We talked and laughed, and I will never forget how important this time was for both of us.

After a few days there, it was time to go and meet the Segur family. We had been in touch with Jessica and her husband who gave us flawless directions on how to get to their place. It was about an hour-and-a-half drive from Orlando, so it wasn't a bad trip at all. Both Holly and I were a little nervous. I mean: here we were going to stay with people we had only spoken to on the phone and never really met.

We pulled up in the driveway and rang the doorbell. Jessica met us at the door with her cute dog Muffin. The minute Jessica looked at us, she knew we were part of the Segur family. Jessica was warm and welcoming and made us both feel at ease right away. We talked for about an hour while we waited for her husband Ernie to come home from work. She said that Holly's eyes were just like those of Madelyn (my supposed birth mother) and that both Holly's and my mannerisms were very similar to Madelyn's. Jessica said that she saw Madelyn in our smiles, in the way that we sat, and in how we both moved our heads and our bodies.

Our visit lasted a few days and was very informative. We learned as much about Madelyn and her family as Jessica could tell us—which was somewhat limited since she really hadn't personally known Madelyn for very long. It was wonderful to meet them, but deep down since there was no positive proof, I still had my doubts. It was not easy saying our good-byes. Jessica said that she would try and come up for a visit to New York to see us again in a few months. We looked forward to seeing her again, but it was never to be.

Once back home, Holly finally made an appointment for the gynecologist and her CAT scan. We were both very happy when the results came back. Not only was there still no sign of cancer; the cyst on her ovary was gone.

During this time in my life, I spent a lot of time reading. I would go with Jayne to the bookstore often, and she would introduce me to many interesting books. Jayne herself was a book collector of sorts and had a huge library of spiritual and metaphysical books. A lot of them she hadn't read, but she had skimmed them and knew basically what they were about. She was able to point out and or tell me about most of the books in the store. I then would have the job of trying to select just one since there were so many I wanted to read. Yet one by one, I learned from these books about the Chakra system, reincarnation, heaven, past lives, automatic writing, psychometry, medicine wheels, meditation, breathing, thi chi, yoga, rituals, moon phases, spirit guides, the symbols of animals and signs of nature—just to name a few. My bookshelf grew and grew.

I began to share my own personal experiences with Jayne and she did the same with me. In doing so, we each gained insight into our personal situations. I began to meet people who were lost and searching like me and was able to help gently suggest, enlighten, and guide them into a new way of thinking. I worked with Jayne at the L.O.V.E. Center leading Medicine Wheel Ceremonies (sessions involving a wheel inside which participants sit and experience 25 different positions in Native American tradition, as personal healing takes place) and many other special workshops that we would work on together. As I grew and in turn others around me grew, I became more confident and secure in my own being and my purpose in life. I was leaving the old me behind and discovering the new and empowered me, the intuitive me, the one who was really connected to God.

My old way of thinking was passing away.

All the blockages and religious fears that had held me back as a child vanished, and new and powerful visions were born.

Do Not Tell Me I Am Dying

We are all dying inside and out.
(Each of us knows that in his own way.
We know ourselves better than our closest friends know us)
Yet we live.
We do not give up hope,
for there is always hope.
Hope for tomorrow, even after death.
Some of us know this feeling of a new life to come.
Some of us have felt this and even seen it on earth.
You do not have to tell me I am dying.
You do not have to tell me that my body is changing
and moving on to a new tomorrow and new beginning.
I am not afraid of what might come
only afraid of what I might miss.
When it comes to be my time,
I want to be able to look in your eyes with the quiet understanding
that we have shared all there is to know between us
for then and only then will I be able to go in peace,
knowing that you will be alright, knowing there was love between us,
knowing we will only be apart for a short period of time.
So do not tell me I am dying
Let us begin today to share our life
like we never have before.

Chapter Eleven

Time moved on with a renewed sense of personal security and peace. I was experiencing a closeness of family, something that I had always longed for. My daughter and I appreciated life and each other more; my mom and I shared our feelings with more ease; and there was a newfound joy for me, as I understood what family happiness was really about. This sense of family unity found me feeling less driven to find absolute proof of who my birth mother was, and this completeness was enhanced with my continuing spiritual growth. The spiritual separation and loneliness that I had felt in the past was decreasing, and I finally knew and felt God's love. I had experienced the power of the mind and how it could transform one's life. I had physically seen loving energy in spiritual form. All of this wrapped around me like a warm security blanket of sorts and allowed me to know that I really was never alone.

The words "we are all a part of God" had new meaning. In the past, I thought that it meant we should believe He was always with us and watching over us, there to guide and protect us, there to receive our prayers and requests for forgiveness. I thought it sinful to assume that we had more control over our lives than we knew and could manifest a life of joy for ourselves. I believe now *that God wants us to find complete happiness and joy. I am not saying that we are God—which is one possible reality, but are we not all part of Him, made in his likeness? Were we not born with the power to bring abundance into our lives, abundance on all levels, such as health, money, love and peace? Can we not do this with positive intent and love? I was beginning to find these truths to be so. I knew it; I had experienced it; and I had created a new life for myself. It certainly had taken a lot of work, trust, and faith, and it was not easy. I had to learn to let go of past fears, fears that had been blocking me from finding my true self, and preventing me from receiving life's true blessings and joy.*

I had come into a time of strength. I had emerged from a time of loss and abandonment. I finally had realized that no matter how lost and lonely we might feel, we are never truly alone. There is always a force of unconditional love watching over us, there to guide and protect us from the pain that we are feeling. We are surrounded by beings— waiting with open arms for us to believe, to let go of our fears, and to receive gentle touches from the Divine. Touches that they eagerly bestow upon us with their hands of love. These are the hands of the angels, the guardians, the guides, and the multitude of spirits who wait in the wing for us to reach out to them with our love so that they, in turn, can reach out to us with theirs.

And so my strength grew, and the day came when my mom sat down to tell me that she had to go into the hospital for bypass surgery. I knew that she was not feeling very well lately and had been to the doctor. Heart problems ran in her family. I was happy that she finally felt comfortable enough to share with me what the doctor had told her. She had already scheduled the surgery and needed someone to take her to the hospital. She asked me if I would do that. Of course I said yes.

The sun hadn't even risen as I rose to pick up my mom on the day that the operation was scheduled. When I arrived at her house, she seemed in good spirits, not that

I expected her to complain in any way, since she had always been a strong person. We arrived at the hospital at around 5:00AM and filled out the intake paperwork; then we sat down and waited for the nurse to tell us that the surgeon was ready. A sweet nun walked by and introduced herself (the hospital was a Catholic institution in which a few nuns remained on-call to speak with patients). She asked my mom what she was there for, and my mother told her that she was going for bypass surgery. The nun held my mom's hands and asked if she could say a prayer; when the pious woman finished, she looked my mother in the eyes, said her good-byes, and told my mom that everything would be all right.

Shortly after the nun left, the nurse called my mom in to prep her for the operation. She said to me that once my mom was ready for surgery, she would call me in to see her one more time before taking her to the operating room. About 20 minutes went by and the nurse called me. She told me that my mom had already been given a shot to relax her and that I could come in and see her until it was time for the operation. I went in and gave my mom a big hug, both of us exchanging that slightly uneasy smile, the kind that you often see in a hospital waiting room. She told me that everything would be fine and said not to worry. I told her that I loved her and knew that she too would be all right. The nurse then appeared, said it was time, and escorted me to the waiting area.

My mom had told me that her boss and builder, Mr. Mario Bummara, would be stopping in to see me and find out how things were going with her. She had worked for him for over 30 years, and he and his family had become a part of ours. He had known my father during the time that Dad was so sick and, honoring my father's wishes, Mr. Bummara had taken on the responsibility of taking care of our family. He had taught my brother and me how to drive, invited us to numerous family gatherings, built a home for my mom at the wholesale cost, hosted my first baby shower, and helped us in every way imaginable. Mom greatly appreciated his love and concern, yet at times found his caring for her a little overwhelming. After all, she had worked hard to become a very independent woman after my father's death.

I waited a little while and then went for a walk outside the hospital. The sun had risen and I knew that I had some time before the doctor would be looking for me. I stumbled upon a simple fenced off area next to the parking lot that was about 10 feet wide and about 200 feet long. It was situated amongst the trees and ran along the edge of the hospital grounds. Entering this cool and comforting area, I saw plaques that represented the "Stations Of The Cross" posted sporadically along the fence. No one else was around, and I wondered how many people knew of this place. I walked along slowly and prayed for my mom, taking in the energy of this peaceful spot. As I reached the last station, I found a beautiful statue of the Virgin Mary nestled amongst ferns and a small pond. She was so beautiful: a tear of hope and a moment of knowing that what was happening was out of my control and in God's hands entered my being. I took a deep breath and closed my eyes, saying one more silent prayer; I turned around to leave this place of solitude and reluctantly went back to the hospital to wait.

Mr. Bummara, or Mr. B. as I called him, came around 11 o'clock and asked me if I would like to go to lunch. Although it was not quite noon, I was hungry, for I had been at the hospital since 5 in the morning. We still had not heard any news about my mom, so I told him that lunch would be nice, and I had a light meal as we sat and exchanged pleasant conversation. We did not linger long and went back to the waiting room to see if there had been any news. The nurse said that my mom was out of the operating room and in recovery and that the doctor would be in to see me. Mr. B. said that he could stay for a while longer. He pledged to keep his eyes and ears out for the doctor if I wanted to close my eyes for a while. I was exhausted, and it probably showed on my face. I thanked Mr. B. and closed my eyes. I felt Mr. B. place his jacket over my shoulders as I drifted in and out of slumber for a while. I woke with him whispering my name, telling me that he had to go, and that he would be back to see my mom later. He asked me if I would be all right. I sat up and told him I would be fine and thanked him for coming as we said our goodbyes. I did not know that this would be the last time I would see him.

Shortly afterward, the nurse came over and told me that my mom's doctor was in the hall waiting to talk to me. I went into the hall and he introduced himself. I had never met him before. He said that the operation was a success but was more difficult than they had expected. He asked me if my mom drank, and I said a little as far as I knew, and he answered by saying that they had to make a larger incision than expected since her spleen was enlarged. He said that it would be sometime before she would be out of recovery and alert enough to talk. He suggested that it would be a good idea, if it appealed to me, to go home and get some rest and come back later.

I had no idea at the time of what I would be in for over the next few days. My mom's recovery was a rough one. The doctors had given her medication to ease her pain— it caused her to hallucinate. Here was my mom, this independent woman, who had a good mind and head on her shoulders, who didn't know where she was and wasn't even able to feed herself. Unattended briefly, she called the police telling them that the hospital was holding her captive. My brother was upset with the situation and wanted to speak to the doctor to find out what was going on. So did Bob and I. It was quite a while before we were able to get the doctor to return our request and speak with us. When he finally did, he took my mom off of the medication, but it took almost 3 days before she could communicate sensibly with us. She had no idea how long it had been since her operation, and it even took her a while to understand where she was and what had happened. I had never experienced anything like this before in my life. I had no idea of what hospital drugs could do to a person, what to expect, or what was even normal.   The uncertainty and discomfort of the whole situation was intensified by my brother who could not understand why other patients had undergone the same operation and were not drugged in such a way. The hospital's reason for doing this, we were told, was that our mom was unusually restless, wanted to leave, and they were trying to keep her calm.

My mom knew before the operation that she would have scars that went down both legs to her knees and up her abdomen, but she had no idea how severe they would be or how long the recovery would take. Since she lived at home by herself and her house was a two-storey, in which she would have to climb stairs, the hospital suggested she go into a nursing home for a while until she became stronger.   There, they said, she would get the proper treatment and care that she needed.

Once mom was in the nursing home that turned out to be near her own home, Mr. B came to see her every day, making sure that she was getting the proper treatment and always asking her if there was anything she needed.

One day when visiting Mom, after she had been in the nursing home a few days, I asked my mother about the most recent visit that Mr. B had made to her. She said that he had stopped by the night before and had let her know that he would miss her for a day since he would be attending a builders' award meeting. He was going to be receiving some kind of award! I woke up the next morning and was getting myself ready for the day when the phone rang. It was Polly, Mr. B's daughter. She told me that the night before, her dad was being given the award, and he just fell down and died of a heart attack.

I was in shock, I couldn't believe my ears.

Polly said that she wanted to tell me right away; she was concerned for my mom and worried about how she would take the news. I told her that I would be careful about how I told her.

I phoned my brother, and together we arranged for a nurse to bring our mother to the lounge area where we would be able to have some privacy, with medical staff on-call, while we told her the news. Gordon met me after work and we went into the nursing home together. My brother and I were very nervous; I knew how close my mom was to Mr. B, and I was not sure how she would react or how this shocking news would affect her in her already weakened health condition.

The nurse brought her to the room. We told my mom that we had some unsettling news. She knew something was up since we had brought her to a private room. She said that she could handle it and would be all right. The nurse said then that she would wait outside and we could call her if we needed her. We told my mom what had happened. She was surprised, yet amazingly strong. She just kept saying that it was so hard for her believe he went so quickly, but told us that he had been having some problems with his heart, something my brother and I weren't even aware of. She felt strong enough for us to take her to the wake to see the family and talk to them.

Our mother eventually recovered, left the nursing home, went back home, but never seemed as strong as she used to be. She still was very independent, and my brother, my husband, and I helped her in whatever way we could. Although she was now in a weakened state, she worked with Polly in the office to settle Mr. Bummara's business (since she handled his books) and helped Polly close down the building company completely.

It was a difficult experience for everyone, but I was filled with gratitude for the new and good rapport that my mom and I had developed before this traumatic ordeal. Our new relationship had allowed her to let go and to trust me with important decisions, as she never had before; with faith, she let me handle things that needed to be done and to help her in anyway I could. This simple energy of trust made me stronger and gave me more confidence in myself. Although I knew what a strong woman Mother was, I looked up to her more than ever, developed more respect for who she was, and admired her perseverance and strength.

Through all of these happenings, I knew that I was never alone. We often look to the heavens for help; we pray and wonder when it will be sent to us. We forget about the many wonderful people in our lives who are there expectedly and unexpectedly for us. These people are sent from heaven, these people are the angels on earth. I have been blessed in life with many special human angels, and Mr. Bummara was no exception.

The L.O.V.E. Center was doing well, and I was meeting new people and becoming aware of other spiritual outlets, healers, psychics, and mediums across the nation and on Long Island. Sylvia Browne was becoming a well-known psychic, and I had scheduled a reading with her. Since she was so well-known it took me a year to get an appointment, but I was willing to wait. I knew of her amazing ability and hoped that she would be able to confirm who my birth family was.

I made up my list of questions and waited patiently by the phone for her call. When the phone finally rang and I found out it was her, I was so excited. It was thrilling to be speaking to her in person. She said that she was sure that I had a lot of questions, but first she wanted to know my full birth name and birthday, and she wanted to give me a few of her own messages.

She started out by asking me if I knew what a life theme was. I had read many of her books, so I knew that she professed that most people were born with two life themes, one that basically represented our life purpose and the other that represented our learning lesson— what we had to work through: our life struggle. She told me that I had a humanitarian life theme and rejection issues that I was almost through. She said that the women's circle would do well, that I was allergic to dairy, that my husband had a back problem, that Holly was stubborn, and that Nick would go into the field of ecology and planetary work. There were a few more things she mentioned before she asked me if I had any questions; then it was time for my list. One at a time, I read the bullets on my list. Essentially this is what she told me: I had found my birth family; my birth mom had been bi-polar and died; my birth father was also dead from an accident; Holly was my mom reincarnated and we had spent many other lifetimes together in France and Egypt. She continued and said that I had many spirits around me, one named Calyn, along with five angels, and that in a meditation, I had been given the gift of healing, and that I should write an autobiography. I thanked her for everything that she had told me, and we said our goodbyes.

More than a year later, during a book signing, Syliva told everyone in line that, with regret, she could not give anyone a message as she signed our respective books. It would take too long, she said. When it was my turn, I walked up to the desk to have my book signed. As I was walking away, she said 'Miss' loudly to get my attention. I turned around; she looked at me, not knowing who I was, and told me again that I should write. I was in shock. She must have really had to give me that message since she had told us that she could not relay any messages before the signing and no one else in that line received a message during the book-signing process. During our prior phone conversation, Sylvia had confirmed many things that I already knew or had suspected. This day, in-person, she again strongly suggested that I should/would write a book.

The information from Sylvia was overwhelming, especially since she had received no prior knowledge about my past or anything about me other than my married name. Sylvia had hit the nail on the head with the part about my mother and daughter, especially about how my mom had died, and she seemed to know everything about my birth family. I had suspected that since Holly: (1) was conceived the same month that my birth mother had died, (2) was born less than an hour to my birth mom's birthday, and (3) shared a physical resemblance with Madelyn Segur, confirmed by the picture whose eyes reflected back my own daughter's face, that there was a chance that Holly could be my birth mother reincarnated. I did not expect this conjecture to be independently reaffirmed by Syliva Browne. Could this really be true, I wondered? One day, when driving in the car, I asked Spirit to give me another sign to confirm what I had heard; within minutes, I got my affirmation. The song "I Knew I Loved You", by Savage Garden came on the radio. The words were profound. I place them here:

Maybe it's intuition, but some things you just don't question.
Like in your eyes, I see my future in an instant
And there it goes, I think I've found my best friend
I know that it might sound more than a little crazy
But I believe

Chorus:
I knew I loved you before I met you
I think I dreamed you into life
I knew I loved you before I met you
I have been waiting all my life.

There's just no rhyme or reason only a sense of completion
And in your eyes, I see the missing pieces; I'm searching for
I think I've found my way home
I know that it might sound more than a little crazy

But I believe

Chorus

A thousand angels dance around you, I am complete now that I found you

Chorus

Waiting all my life? This life maybe I was waiting to know my birth mom, *yet she had been* with *me all along; she had been with me in other lifetimes, like Egypt and France, as Sylvia had said. I had forgotten, and now I remembered. Something within my soul told me this was true. All of this hit me hard, and tears came to my eyes: I had been searching all my life for my mom, and here she was, right by my side since the birth of my daughter. I told my daughter of all this and she didn't blink an eye. She too knew within herself that it was all true. I thought this to be amazing and was not aware at the time that there would be more messages from Spirit that would come.*

I had been asking my friends if they knew of anyone who was good at cutting hair. My friend Jayne and Karen (Jayne's friend and a woman who later took dance lessons from me) had gone to a salon run by lady who was a member of the L.O.V.E. Center. They said that she was very good at cutting hair, so I decided to make an appointment with her. Everyone called her Cookie, even though her name was Renata. I was very happy with what she did with my hair and continued to choose her as my stylist. As time went on, we became very good friends. Since she belonged to the Center, we had all sorts of spiritual things to talk about. I talked her into coming for dance lessons, which she thoroughly enjoyed. Cookie's astrological sign was Pisces and so was mine. We were the same age and our birthdates were the same month. We would tease each other now and then—me telling her that I was the big fish (the symbol of Pisces being the two fish swimming) and she the little fish—and she would come back and say once in a while that she was the big fish and I the small. We got along well, and over the years, we spent much time laughing, meditating, and talking together. Through meditation, we even found ourselves going back in time to other lives that we had spent together. I loved Cookie's company for I was to find what a brave and spiritual being she truly was. She always had a smile on her face and was full of life. I found out that she had endured a rough ongoing battle with breast cancer, and when my daughter was sick, Cookie was a great source of inspiration and comfort to me. She never really spoke much about her illness, but in time I found out that she had been through a mastectomy, had gone into remission, had changed her diet holistically and had done everything she could to improve her health, all with that ever-constant spiritual energy that she possessed. I would tell people that she was an angel and an amazing human being who set an example of spiritual strength and courage.

One day, Cookie said that one of the Presbyterian churches near us was having a labyrinth walk. I had heard of a labyrinth, but had never had the chance to experience one. I told her that I would go with her to the event. As we walked into the building, there on the floor, was a labyrinth painted on canvas. I had to wonder what kind of spiritual peace I would receive from this painted object laying on the floor. The woman who was running the event was very informative. She told us that the labyrinth was over 4,000 years old and was a meditative path. You could easily meditate as you walked it since, unlike a maze, it didn't have any wrong turns or dead ends.

The way in was the way out.

After the woman's short lecture, it was time for each of us to walk. One by one we entered this sacred geometric shape, leaving enough space between each person as not to crowd each other. At first I didn't feel anything, and then suddenly I began to feel a tremendous sense of peace. It was so strong that it almost brought tears to my eyes. I then saw a vision of myself building my own labyrinths for other people. This was an inspiring revelation for me, in view of the fact that I had been searching for something creative and spiritual that I could do with my time, given that I was no longer doing the dance studio stage production work. I had missed the challenge of creating something from scratch and the labyrinth seemed to be the perfect solution to regaining some of my creativity. I was so excited. I had never expected to get so much out of what I thought was going to be a simple walk. Cookie too thought the experience was extraordinary.

Within a year, I created my first labyrinth at the L.O.V.E. Center, using tape on the floor. At least twice a year, from that point on, I have created a labyrinth, either indoors or outdoors, anywhere from 30 to 72 square feet in size. Over the years, I have used, tape, cord, crepe paper, Christmas and black lights to create multiple labyrinth shapes. Some have also had bonfires in their center, others candles, special lighting, or a pyramid placed in its middle. Each one was individual in its own way, and each person that entered had his or her own spiritual experience. Cookie tried never to miss a walk.

Giving to others was always something I enjoyed doing, and now I was able to express myself, not only blossoming in creativity again, but in spirituality as well.

Part of me could not understand why I had such an affinity for creating labyrinths. It was interesting that although I had considered math a weakness, I was flourishing when it came to geometry. Even my teachers in high school could not understand that. Had I done something like this before in a past life, I wondered? What other reason would there be for this unusual gift. All this was made clear to me one day during a soul reading that Ellie (my friend, a trans-channeler[1], and the lady who founded the L.O.V.E. Center) gave me. She said that I had lived in the Hanging Gardens of Babylon in Old Testament times. I was blind, was one of the few people permitted in the catacombs, and I knew their complicated ins and outs. In another recent channeling, Ellie told me that I had helped create many labyrinths in the past by infusing the structure with scared energy. It was clear to me after learning this that my gift of sacred geometry stemmed from past lifetime experiences that were unforgotten memories and part of my soul essence.

Presenting a labyrinth brought me closer to God, for I felt joyful as I watched each person walk each

---

[1] Trans-channeler: A trans-channeler is similar to a person who channels. A channeler is a person who, while in a meditative state, will bring in messages from The Other Side (spirits, angels, masters, guides, loved ones who have passed, and teachers) and most of the time remembers what has happened during the time he or she is in meditation. Such channelers normally do not leave their bodies or allow entities to use their bodies as a vehicle of communication. However, a trans-channeler will not remember anything that happened during the meditative session since he or she seems to go somewhere else, actually leaving the body and often times allowing other entities to use the trans-channeler's body as a vehicle for communication. Trans-channelers will not remember the meditative sessions and will have to be told what went on during it. Note: We always record Ellie's sessions so we can review and transcribe them for our group members to read.

spiritual creation. The visual beauty of each individual carrying his own candle—his light—each representing a parallel personal connection to Spirit, strengthened my heart. The joy and appreciation that each person expressed brought new meaning into my life. I, at last, had found a new purpose for my talents and creativity and I knew deep within my soul that this spiritual gift fulfilled me in ways that I could hardly express. The joyfulness that I felt, as I watched each person walk these scared geometric shapes, reflected upon my life and helped me realize how right Syliva Browne was: I truly was a humanitarian. I knew that now. I could feel it in my soul. I saw the beauty and joy that I had brought into other people's lives not only through the labyrinth walks, but also through the dance lessons over the years: dozens of children and adults spiritually and physically enriched. My life had been worthwhile; I wasn't a worthless human being; what I did and who I was counted for something in this world, and the recognition of that touched me profoundly. The fear of death was no longer an issue in my life. I knew that those who had gone before me were now in a better place, and I felt that between the gifts that I had been given and my renewed strength (valuing my own life), I could die knowing that I had come into this world and made a difference to others in some way.

This spiritual strength I had developed kept me sturdy through the death of my (and Jayne's) friend Karen It helped me hold Cookie's hand and give her strength as she became more and more ill, and together we walked one more labyrinth. These two beautiful women, although they died young, had left their marks on the world as they touched so many hearts. To this day, I can sense their presence and connect with them in my dreams. Although they are no longer on this earth plane, I know they are both beside me, watching over me, and guiding me in all that I do. I know my birthmother and father are with me, protecting me with their love and guidance, which never ends even from beyond.

One day, Bob and I were painting the shed in the backyard and my mom stopped by for a visit. She had some wonderful news. She had gone to a hypnotist's class a few weeks ago and wanted to tell us that it had been three weeks and she had not had one cigarette. We were shocked and were so proud of her, since she had smoked from the time that she was a young girl. From that day, my mom never picked up another cigarette, but continued unfortunately to have breathing problems.

The harsh consequence of this life of smoking hit home one day in the doctor's office when I was with my mom. The doctor came into the room to tell us that he had the results of her tests, and they had found a tumor in her lung. He said that she was breathing only up to 20% of her capacity, and in her condition and at her age, there was no guarantee that she could survive any kind of operation. He had no idea how or if this tumor would progress and started her on an inhaler and other medications to help her condition. This was in the fall of 2000. The holidays were approaching, and I wondered what the rest of that year or the next would bring. Few words were spoken between my mom and me. We both knew what this meant; we did not need to mull over the facts.

Being the efficient woman my mom was, she continued to prepare her home, something she felt was important to do, by labeling and writing notes on all of her things; this was so in the case of her death, my brother and I would not be left unaware or wondering where things came from, what they were, and how valuable they might be. Mom even decided that it was time to go to the funeral home, settle what she wanted done with her body, and pay for any expenses in advance so this too my brother and I would not have to worry about. All of this was done and put in detailed writing. She even added on this paper her bank account, doctors, and all other important information that we might need in case of her death. Something I hope to do for my children too.

During the end of the year I had a chance to talk to my mom about the house and told her that I certainly did not want to suggest that she had to leave her home, but if it was getting to be too much, maybe together we could look into an apartment or assisted living facility for her. At the time she listened, but I could tell that it was a decision she was not wanting to think about or face. The holidays came and I wanted them to be extra special. Something inside of me, although I had no way of knowing, wondered if this would be my last Christmas with my mom. I kept this to myself, which might not have been such a good idea.

Our small family was all together that year except for my daughter who got delayed at a friend's house and wasn't going to be able to get home until later, unfortunately after the rest of the family had left. My daughter was thinking that everyone would be staying later, but my mom was tired and not up to making it a late night. In the long run, Holly did not get to spend Christmas with my mom, who was very upset, and my brother was quite angry with Holly too. There wasn't anything I could do at the time. However, later on, after my mom's death, my daughter told me that she wished she had known how sick her grandmother really was, and she would have tried to make more of an effort to be there with her that year. Holly has struggled with the emotions and regrets of not being there that Christmas, but has had Divine messages that have told her that my mom forgives her and is by her side.

My mother's breathing worsened, and the doctor told her that he wanted to put her on oxygen. She was not happy. The idea of carrying around a tank did not thrill her. She told the doctor that she was doing fine. He told her that it would help her and that he was ordering it for her and asked her to at least use it at night, which she reluctantly did. My brother looked into a smaller unit that would be easier for her to carry, and as time went on she herself realized that she needed the oxygen more and more.

Eventually she said to me that she thought she would look into another place to live and asked me if I would go with her. We looked into some other apartments, but most were very expensive. Together, we finally found an assisted living home which she liked and started making plans for her move. She set up the sale of her house and it sold in a week. Closing was going to be taking place the beginning of April.

It was the end of February 2001 when my mom signed the papers and made a date for Thursday, March 22nd to move into her new home. My mom and I had spent the last few weeks packing things carefully. It was very difficult for her, since she was going from a huge house to a single room. She could only take a few special things; most had to go. I labeled boxes of antiques, clothes, knick-knacks, pots and pans, kitchen supplies etc. so we would know what she had. The plan was that my mom would look through one box at a time after the move and tell me what she wanted me to do with each.

On my 50th birthday, on March 17th 2001, the whole family was together for a special dinner out. We had a fantastic time and were set for my mom's big move that Wednesday. Although it was a day earlier than they told my mom she could move in, the facility was fine with us bringing mom's things there to set them up. So on March 21st, Gordon, Bob, Mike (a friend of ours), Holly, Nick, and I were all there with the truck we rented. My mom packed a few more things while we loaded the truck, brought her things to the room and set everything up for her. The only things that would come later would be her food, some pots and pans, final pieces of clothing, and plants.

On Thursday the 22nd, she had her final medical intake at the assisted living home. She had been weak for some time and had been walking more slowly. Most times, when she went out, she would not use her oxygen. That day was no exception. I noticed that she was moving more slowly than normal and had to stop a few times to catch her breath. To be honest, I didn't think that much about it, since I figured it was due to her not using the oxygen while she was out. After she had seen the doctor, I asked her if she felt up to going up to her room and seeing how we had set things up for her. She said yes. She entered the room and sat down and looked around and said, "Is this where I will be living?" I told her yes and asked her if she liked it. She was amazed at how beautiful everything looked and impressed by all the work we had done.

I was a little taken back by her question, knowing that she did know she was moving in and wondering why she would ask me if this was where she was living. Again I let it go.

The following morning early she called me and said that she had had a problem getting to the bathroom and needed me to come by and help her. I went over to help her clean up. She was too weak to handle any big cleaning jobs at this point in her life and was very concerned that the house be left in perfect condition for the new owners who would be moving in. I got her settled and asked her if she needed anything. She said she was fine and was tired and was going to rest.

The next morning, Saturday March 24th, my mom called again. This time she told me that she had made a bigger mess at the house and was very upset. I told her I would be right over. Bob was home, so he went with me. I helped her clean up the floor and herself and asked her how long she had been having this problem. She said about a week. I said mom this is serious and called my brother telling him that I was taking her to the hospital.

On the way to the hospital, my mom told me that she had been seeing angels. My heart jumped, for I didn't want to face what I knew that might mean. I didn't want to think that they had been there preparing her and calling her home.

The emergency room took her information and they got her a bed, checked her vital signs, which were fine and told me that she was just very dehydrated. I was happy to hear that her condition was OK. My brother and his girlfriend Carol arrived, and I told Carol that my mom had said she had seen the angels; Carol gasped. I continued by saying the doctors said that she was all right and that she would have to stay in the hospital for a while.   After also explaining to the doctors about mom's breathing condition and problems, we were asked if we had considered hospice care. I told the doctors that we had her set up to move into an assisted living home on Monday. They said it would be a while before they could get her a room at the hospital.

I called the kids to tell them what was happening; it was unusual, but both of them were home. I told them what had happened to nana and that the doctors seem to think she was fine, that she was going to have to stay in the hospital and that I would call them as soon as they got her in a room and they could then come and visit her. They said all right.

My mom tossed and turned, trying to get comfortable, sleeping on and off. While keeping her as comfortable as possible, we talked to her a little here and there when she would wake up. Holly and Nick showed up unexpectedly; they said that they had talked and together decided they should come to the hospital. When they walked in, and my mom saw them, she sat up in bed with a smile. She was so happy to see them and it was the most amount of energy I had seen her express in days. Holly and Nick's nana spent a little time talking to each of them and then the nurse appeared to take her vitals again. She said that she was doing well and left the room. Mom felt tired again and lay down to close her eyes. A minute or two went by and she wanted us to help her move to get comfortable again. With Gordon on one side and myself on the other, as we carefully tried to turn her and adjust her pillows, my mother took a deep breath and feel asleep forever. I knew what had happened, and I looked at my family, and said I think she has passed. I told Gordon to get the nurse. None of us could totally believe it, but it was confirmed by the nurse that she had gone home. Holly felt like she couldn't breathe and said she was going out for air. I went after her and the rest of the family followed. Once outside we held each other and cried.

I was surprised that she had passed, given the fact that her vital signs had been good, but I was glad that the kids for some reason had felt the need to come to the hospital, that her close family members were there, and that she went peacefully.

Gordon and I went to the funeral parlor to tell the funeral director that our mother had passed and to make sure that they knew what type of service my mom wanted. They found her paperwork and told us that she wanted to be cremated, have a one-day memorial service and be buried with my father. We arranged that all to take place in two days, knowing we needed the time to call everyone about her passing, including the assisted living home.

That night I had a dream that my brother and I were in the hospital waiting room. My mom was there on an office swivel chair and she looked beautiful. She was pushing herself around the room on the chair and spinning happily. She looked at me and told me to tell my brother that she was fine and then floated away through the wall of the room. I told my brother the next day as we were looking through pictures for the memorial services about my dream. I don't think he knew what to make of it. As we were looking through all these hundreds of pictures I came across four that were of her, taken in the office where she worked and looking just like I had seen her in my dream. I wondered how old she was then, for I vaguely remembered her looking that way. When I turned over one of the pictures to see if there was a date on the back, all that was on it was 1969. I gasped, my heart leapt; I was touched and it was definitely a sign. My mom had never remarried since my father's death in 1969 for she always loved him. This sign and event was my mother's way of letting me know she was in heaven with my dad.

Things were rough for a while for my brother, for my family, and for me. We had a lot to do in a short time. We had to move all of my mother's things out of the assisted living home that Wednesday, one week after we had moved everything in; we had her house to empty since the people were going to be moving in at the beginning of the month; we needed to sell her car, sort out what we were probably keeping, donate some of mom's things to charity, and move the rest to our homes where we would have more time to sort through the valuables at a later date. I think what amazed me the most about all of this is how my brother and I worked together. Yes, we both had some different ideas, but we were able to communicate better than we had in years and get through all that had to be done with great respect, love, and understanding of each other's feelings. Although we both felt the loss of our mother deeply, it was a blessing to have each other to hold on to during this time.

There have been many moments since then that I have felt my mom's presence. I feel her watching over me, guiding me, protecting me and even once-in-a-while telling me to be careful, just the way she would if she were still physically in my life. My daughter also had experiences with her nana being around; like the time Holly was talking about her and the television went on and off a few times. It is a comfort to me to have developed this sense of attunement, and even though I have a slight twinge of abandonment, having lost two sets of parents, I spiritually know that their love surrounds me, not only on the earth plane, but from beyond as well.

My friends and I had set a date to go and see an artist and psychic named Daniel Akner. My husband Bob was supposed to be a part of our group, but he could not make it that evening. I took the picture of my birth mom with me in hopes that I might be able to receive a confirmation from Daniel that she was my mom. We arrived at his home and he went right to work using his amazing gift and his beautifully hand-painted tarot cards. He began by saying that he would take some time to see who might come in to deliver a message to us. He said that he had a message for me for someone named Robert. I almost laughed. My husband's name was Robert and like I said, he was supposed to be there and couldn't make it. Here Daniel was giving me a message for him anyway. He told me that he was watched over by his grandfather and that although it could be very dangerous going in and out of New York since the 9 / 11 incident, he needed not worry. It was very comforting to know that my husband was Divinely protected.

Daniel spent time with each of my other friends giving them amazing messages from Spirit. At last, it was time for each of us to ask a question if we wished. When it was my turn, I took out the picture of Madelyn and placed it on the table. I asked Daniel if he could tell me if this woman in the picture was my birth mother. He said, well let's see about that, and he shuffled his cards then pulled one blindly from the deck. Silence. Then: "The answer is a definite 'Yes,'" he said with conviction. The photo that I had showed Daniel, **was indeed** of my birth mom, Daniel affirmed, since the card that he had drawn was the only card in the deck like this: it was a picture of a mother and her child. But even more unusual: "This particular and extraordinary card hasn't always been in my deck," he said, "because I originally painted it to give to my mother when her mother was dying, so even when my grandma passed, my mother would always know that her mother was with her—and my grandma would feel the same. Before my own mom became ill and died," Daniel continued, "she gave this card back to me so that I would always know that she was with me."

I was overwhelmed and touched. I knew he was right that this was my birth mother. What other explanation could there be for this particular card to be drawn from the deck.

Since that day at Daniel's house, I have not wanted or cared to look further for confirmation of my birth mom. It was such a moving experience that I know its deep meaning, and truth was given to me from the Spirit world. That evening Daniel also told me that when my daughter was ill, she had three women watching over her throughout the ordeal and that Madelyn was one of them.

As I end this chapter, I am sure that some of you are wondering how Holly could be protected by Madelyn when Holly was Madelyn's reincarnation. I am still pondering this question myself. There are still many things in this life that we do not thoroughly understand, one of them being time and space, or past, present and future. Could they all exist simultaneously? One idea behind Wave Theory is that maybe the future is also the past. An example of this would be if you took a cord and stretched it out between two people, each person holding one end, then one person snaps the cord making a wave that moves down the cord to the other person. From there that wave bounces off that person and returns to the person who snapped the cord. This wave moving out is the future and the wave coming back is basically returning to the past. People have been asking; "Does Time Exist?" No one has proven it one way or the other.

A Spiritualist once said that time is a built-in concept that we alone are born to perceive in order to measure things in our lives. However maybe Time itself exists on many levels and is multidimensional? I do not want to take up a lot of time here, for this is not the point of the book, but if time does not exist, maybe we are in a constant flow of love and protection, from the past, present and future, where our children can protect us as well as we can protect them, where they are not only in our lives now on this plane, but they are the circle (or cycle) of family and love that coexists together and never ends.

*Pieces of paper folded together
to make one striking design.
That is how life can be.
Separate pieces of paper
each one of its own essence
joining in one perfect design
to form a beautiful piece of artwork.
Like the famous painters,
we can each make a faultless masterpiece.
Paint your way through life
in all your color and glory
until you have created a canvas of exquisiteness.
Take up your pens, brushes, chalk,
or whatever instruments you want to use
and make your world a magnificent place to live in.*

Chapter Twelve

I believe that we all are born with the gift of insight.

This innate trait and ability that we hold within can propel us through our world freely, bringing us blessing and much peace. We are always connected to the Other Side, and when we honor this connection—aligning in full awareness with our inborn gifts and senses, we are transformed.

[Such transformation occurs and is revealed as we practice and work with our abilities, tuning into our souls and into the grace of all the universal powers that be. In return for our practice and our work, those Powers answer our questions, guide us, protect us, and bring abundance into our lives.]

All of this has been an amazing journey, as I have progressed through my life with an open mind, increasingly heeding my intuition and discovering new truths. In the beginning, I wasn't sure of how much, if at all, my life could change based merely on indulging intuition, but now that I have lived and experienced: (1) my gifts, (2) Divine Intervention, and (3) more abundance and peace in my life, I realize how disconnected I was and I humbly thank the Force (the All That Is) for helping me.

In this chapter, I would like to tell my readers about some of the wonderful experiences I have had in my life as I discovered, connected with, and used my gifts. Or to put it another way, as I tuned into and honored my intuition. You will find that although I have divided these experiences into sections, some of them will naturally overlap and blend. Each has its untraditional title along with its more well-known appellation in parenthesis. This is my way of adding a little levity into the book and hopefully increasing many readers' enjoyment.

~

As I Lay Me Down To Sleep (Dreams)

My *dreams* at night have given me much insight, answered questions, given me solutions to problems, and connected me to those who have passed. Dreams were one of the first gifts that I discovered that I had within me. To benefit from this gift, all I had to do was ask questions, and practice writing down the answers that I would receive in the night. After a while, I would remember my dreams more readily and be able to look up their meaning if I was not sure about it. (Two of my favorite books for dream interpretation are: T*he Mystical Magical Marvelous World of Dreams* by Wilda B. Tanner and *Mary Summer Rain's Guide to Dream Symbols* by Mary Summer Rain and Alex Greystone; both works seem to have a Spiritual flair.) With some of my dreams, there was no question of meaning.

Shortly after Deanna (my dance student) passed away, I experienced a series of three dreams, or messages. At first I thought it was just my imagination; but after the third dream, I knew I had to mention these visions to my former student's family. In one dream, I saw little Deanna wearing white gloves; in another, I was knitting a blanket in a church as she sat next to me; in the last, my young dance student came to me and kept repeating the following message over and over, keeping me awake for what seemed like—and may well have been—half the night: "Please Tell My Family That I Am Fine." Although each dream was a little bit different, they all had that one thing in common: at the end, Deanna would gently say to me "Please Tell My Family That I Am Fine."

I chose to ignore the first two dreams, since I did not know how the family would react if I told them about these dreams, but by the time I received the third one, there was no question in my mind that I had to tell one of the family members. I spoke to Deanna's sister, Angie. She was grateful for the message and she revealed to me that Deanna wore white gloves when she was buried, something I was not aware of. Since that message was delivered, I have not had another dream about Deanna.

Rascal, one of our cats, was very special to us. We had bought him from LAP (League of Animal Protection). He was two years old, and when we first encountered him, he was the only cat hanging upside down on top of a shelf. He took to our kids immediately. We knew by his demeanor that he would be a very gentle and loving cat, which turned out to be true. Around eleven years old, Rascal began to get sick, and upon taking him to the vet, we discovered that although he had received his feline leukemia shots every year, he had developed the disease. Since we did not know Rascal's original health history (he had joined our family at two years old) or that cats can have the disease at birth laying dormant in their immune systems, we were shocked. Rascal went downhill quickly and towards the end, although I had never had to do this before with any creature, we put him to sleep since he was so sick and not eating. It was one of the hardest things I ever had to do, and I struggled with the fact, as I am sure others do, that we— rather than (in any immediately obvious way) *God*—had by our decision triggered the timing of our pet's passing. Bob and I held each other and cried half the night until I finally fell asleep.

I dreamed about Rascal that night. He was in a park with other animals, and they were all playing and running and having a wonderful time. Rascal was running up a slide from the bottom to the top and then jumping off, having a great time. He did this over and over in my dream, and I could see how happy he was. In the days after waking, I told a few people about the dream, but wasn't totally convinced of its meaning until I received an email from a concerned friend with the following message, a few days after Rascal's death. It touched my heart and brought peace again to my life:

Rainbows Bridge
Author Unknown

Just this side of heaven is a place called Rainbow Bridge.
When an animal dies that has been especially close to someone here,
that pet goes to Rainbow Bridge.
There are meadows and hills for all of our special friends
so they can run and play together.
There is plenty of food, water, and sunshine,
and our friends are warm and comfortable.
All the animals who had been ill and old
are restored to health and vigor.
Those who were hurt or maimed are made whole and strong again,
just as we remember them in our dreams of days and times gone by.
The animals are happy and content,
Except for one small thing:
They miss someone very special to them,

who had to be left behind.

They all run and play together, but the day comes when one suddenly
stops
and looks into the distance.
His bright eyes are intent.
His eager body quivers.
Suddenly he begins to run from the group,
flying over the green grass,
his legs carrying him faster and faster.
You have been spotted,
and when you and your special friend finally meet,
you cling together in joyous reunion,
never to be parted again.
The happy kisses rain upon your face;
your hands again caress the beloved head,
and you look once more into the trusting eyes of your pet,
so long gone from your life,
but never absent from your heart.
Then you cross Rainbow Bridge together...

~

Over the years, I have had dreams that I know have deep
meaning and are very profound. Some of these dreams
are strange and unreal. In one such recurring dream, I
am able to walk under water: very unusual. As I am
doing this in the dream, I am using no special breathing
apparatus and the process seems totally natural to me. I
decided one day at one of my reunion trips to Virginia
that I would ask Ellie, who was trans-channeling the
Force (All That Is) at the time, what the dream meant.
She told me that the imagery and associated full
experience in my dream was rooted deeply in a past life.

In that life, I was a Lemurian[2]. The people, at the time of Lemuria, could walk unaided under the water. It was interesting; was I actually experiencing or revisiting one of my past lives? Maybe that is why this particular recurring dream felt so real and natural to me.

~

Coming Attractions *(Precognition)*

When I was a teenager, I began to see events before they happened. It was like a movie flashing before my eyes. At first, I had no idea what was happening to me; usually within moments after, the envisioned incident would occur. Over time, I would try to stop what I saw from happening, but found most of the time I was too late. The first time was when my boyfriend and brother were wrestling in the back yard, and I saw my boyfriend falling on a partially hidden pair of scissors that were on the ground. Within moments, he fell and landed on the scissors, putting their sharp point into his arm. Another time, my brother was playing with a glass ashtray and in a more powerful manner than mere imagination, I saw and felt him dropping it and breaking it; right after this pre-cognized experience, it happened. Having this ability did not feel inspiring or even positive to me since I could not seem to prevent what was going to happen and I felt helpless, so I chose not to work with it and tried to push anything I saw aside. Since I have not worked with this gift in a long time, I rarely see events before they happen.

---

[2] (Lemuria is often described as the location where Adam and Eve went after the Garden of Eden; it was a series of islands that extended from Hawaii all the way down to Easter Island. Lemuria sank during a change in the axis of the earth and at the same time that Atlantis rose.)

~

Touched By An Angel (Divine Intervention)

There are many times that I have been protected in my life. During these moments, it was clear that angels were watching over me and protecting me. I am sure that many readers too have stories to tell about moments in which they know there was no other way that they could have escaped death without being touched by an angel.

Driving back and forth to college was a normal thing for me to do in my Chevy Impala. It was a second-hand car that my mom had picked up for me so that I could get to school. I was on my way home one beautiful day, feeling the Divine order of everything, when all of a sudden, I noticed the car was picking up speed and my foot was not on the gas. It was a two-lane country road with no shoulder, and the car in front of me was about three car-lengths away. I stepped on the brake. I kept pressing on the brake. It went to the floor and did nothing. My car and my surroundings continued to pick up speed, and at this point, I was doing about 40 miles-an-hour. I saw that the road was widening up ahead and thought I could pull over and pull on the emergency break. As I rounded the corner and looked to the side, parked along the edge of the road was an eighteen-wheeler. At this point, I was doing 45 and, God willing, I decided to pull in front of the semi-truck noticing that the steering on my car was off. I pulled on the emergency break and it did nothing. As I looked up, there was a fence to my right, a "One Way" sign next to it, and a telephone pole next to that. I didn't have time to think; based only very loosely on my intense interaction with the steering wheel, the car pulled in-between the fence and the pole, hitting the "One Way" sign with a jolt that stopped the car. I had no idea what had happened. I phoned my mother from a nearby house, and she called a tow truck and came right out to assist me. The tow truck operator opened the hood of my car and showed my mom what had happened. He said that the engine mounts had broken and pulled the brake-line hose, leaving me with no brakes at all. It also had pulled the automatic steering line, which is why the car was so hard to steer. The tow truck man looked at my mom and told her that her daughter was a very lucky lady, for I was only about one inch away from the fence and the telephone pole, and he said that he probably couldn't have parked the car between them if he tried.

> *Many years later, the following thought occurred to me: it is almost as if the "One Way" sign, which single-handedly broke the car's out-of-control momentum, was truly a sign of multiple meanings. It literally, figuratively, and metaphysically was a sign reminding me that there is only **One** way that my car could have found this path to the only safe location nestled perilously amongst danger on both sides and chaos under its own hood. There is only One energy and only one genuinely fulfilling **way** of loving life and everything in it—the way of* **unconditional** *love.   That One way might also be called God—or, All That Is.*

As nerves gradually calmed, my mom asked the tow truck guy what I could have done to control the car in such a situation. He said 'nothing,' except maybe turn the car off and put it in low gear. I thanked God that I wasn't at all hurt and felt divinely protected, especially that I hadn't pulled off the road behind the eighteen-wheeler.

Three months later, my mom was driving down the road and had the same thing happen to her car. She was saved since she knew what to do thanks to what had happened to me and thanks to Divine intervention striking again.

~

Pump Up The Volume (Channeling & Mediumship)

That small 'voice' within can be very powerful. Most of the time we just ignore it, thinking it is just our random thoughts or wanderings of the mind. As I gradually learned to pay more attention to what my mind was saying, I realized that what was really happening was: Spirit was trying to get my attention and speak to me. Have you ever heard your name called only to turn around to an empty room? Maybe a long lost relative or spirit guide was trying to speak to you. In such (possibly confusing or unnerving) situations, do we ever stop to ask the gentle energy what it wants to tell us? If we did, we might be surprised at the answer. I never thought that I could connect to the Spirit world—or with my guide—until I started to pay more attention to what I was receiving with all my senses. An example follows.

I was in a class working with a large group of people. The teacher had divided us into small groups of four. We were to go into meditation and give messages to each other if possible. I quieted my mind and saw a picture of a pewter heart. I asked the group if someone had given them a heart. One woman said that her mom, who had passed, had given her exactly such an object. Again, I went into a meditative state, this time receiving the picture of an old glass Dunking Duck. This was something I had seen only as a child. It was a glass-weighted duck that would sit on the edge of a glass, tipping to drink out of its contents. I felt funny seeing this at first and had no idea if I should say anything or if I could even explain it. I asked the group if it meant anything to them or if they even knew what I was talking about. The girl whose mom had died told me that she knew exactly what I was talking about because it was her mother's favorite toy. The girl was touched and I learned that no message received is stupid.

Unexpectedly, one night, I dreamed that my daughter was auditioning for a part in a musical. In the dream, the show's director not only declined to give my daughter a part, but he gave all of the singing and acting roles to one person. In the dream, my daughter was upset about this, so I went to the director to try and convince him that since the one person had all the lines in the show, maybe he could audition others to at least sing some of the music. He agreed to the auditions. The day of the auditions, my daughter was waiting for her name to be called, so she could go out on stage to sing her song. I was there with her, and when her name was called, she told me that she wasn't feeling well, and she passed out on the floor. Although at the time she could not speak, she telepathically told me that I should go and sing the song. I told her that I didn't even know it or how it went. She said, "You can do it Mom." I went out on the stage, and to my surprise, I started to sing. The words were beautiful, and I saw myself in a white flowing gown floating above the stage as I sang. I sang the song over and over again in order to remember it, and when—in conscious real life—I woke up, I was able not only to remember the melody, but three verses and the chorus, which follow:

Come To Me Heaven

Channeled by Christine Guardiano

We believe in our hearts, that the earth can transform.
We believe in God's love, for it can be reborn.
For within each soul's heart, is an essence that lives,
That can change what's around us to All That Is.

With the touch of this essence, All life can transform,
If we hold on to love, from the night until morn,
If we pledge to be strong, and ignore all life's scorn,
Then the angels in heaven, will open the door.

Chorus
Come to me heaven, to earth and the sky,
Come to me heaven, from days that passed by.
Let the earth feel your glory, from years long ago,
Let us see all your essence in the new fallen snow.

The door into peace, the door into life,
The door where we all… will have no more strife.
For a new day depends, on each mother and son,
To embrace one another, then a new day will come

~

A Blast From The Past (Past Life Regression)

During the first part of my life, I don't think that I believed in reincarnation or in past lives. However, over the years, I have found that many people whom I personally know have been helped by professionals who can regress them back to their pasts to further understand who they are and help them improve their daily lives. The book *Journey Of The Souls* by Michael Newton, Ph.D, is a wonderful book about the miracles of regression.

Walt Whitman High School was giving a class on Past Life Regression. I had heard about it and was interested, so I went to the class with a friend. I wasn't quite sure how the lady who was running the class would take 40 people back to their pasts all at once, but she did. I had an interesting experience as she brought the class through a guided meditation. I vividly saw myself walking down a street in a city by myself. There was no one around; brownstone buildings lined each side of the street; I was about 12 years old and wearing a blue dress with an apron. I wondered where all the people had gone and then saw myself walking into one of the brownstone buildings to find children sitting along the edge of the room and adults talking in the middle. After listening to their conversation for a while, I realized that I was at a funeral. Once out of the meditative state, I thought to myself: wow, I really have some imagination. When I told my accompanying friend about my imagined experience, she said that she went to the same place as I, and that she had seen me there even though I had not seen her. I didn't know what to think of all this and had trouble sleeping that night. Finally, after tossing and turning that evening, I got up to put on the television and found an old black and white movie on. I don't remember the movie, but when I saw the street lamps, I was blown away because they looked precisely like the ones from my regression. I no sooner wondered what time period this depicted when the year '1902' came upon the screen. To this day, I have rarely seen a movie flash just the year on the screen. I felt Spirit was giving me a confirmation that this was one of my past lives.

For over fifteen years (in my present lifetime), I had experienced trouble with my digestion. During a particular past life regression, I saw/experienced myself as a male native foraging the forest for food. I was in a line with my other tribesmen, and we were picking bugs off the leaves and eating them

After this regression, the woman who ran it said that we could share what we saw or call her and speak to her at any time. I listened to others' experiences and kept mine to myself at the time. I was trying to figure out if the reason for my current earthly digestion problems was somehow rooted in eating bugs during a past life.

About a week later, I spoke to the regression therapist about my digestive problems and the regression. She listened to what I had to say and then told me that she felt that the reason for my problems did not stem from the bugs, but from the fact that I was the leader of this tribe and felt guilt because I could not save them, hence the stomach problems—the stomach is one place in the body where guilt often is experienced physically.

~

Sign, Sign, Everywhere A Sign
(Meditation & Symbology)

I believe that the cosmic universe connects to/with us in multiple ways.

As I have said, we all hold many gifts within us that can be activated at any time; however, we are also individuals, and as we begin to open to The Force (All That Is), we will often fully develop one gift, learn something about other gifts and other people's gifts, and experience our own abilities increasing as our lives progress. During our life journeys, Spirit uses its power in whatever way it can to connect to the sense or senses that we have developed, at the appropriate times in our lives. For example, my first developed sense was my dreams, and Spirit used them to send me many messages. As I developed further, my vibrational essence increased; this enabled me to notice and receive the numerous signs that Spirit was sending me. It is not easy sometimes to be attuned to the many messages that are sent to us daily. We all lead very busy lives. This is why meditation is so important. It gives us a chance to center and ground ourselves to receive these messages.

One day, I was coming out of a meditation and, upon opening my eyes, I saw a large grid floating in the air around the room. I blinked my eyes a few times, thinking that my eyelashes were making interesting designs, to find instead that this grid was still there floating around me. It looked like a three-dimensional honeycomb that was drawn by a magic artist in the air. I had no idea of what I was seeing, but was told later that I was seeing the air around me in its natural essence. This was a sign to me that we are all a lot more than what we perceive with our own eyes. Over time, I have been able to connect and draw many of nature's grids the way that I see them through my soul's eyes.

Jayne and I were in meditation one evening at the Center. She was traveling to the higher planes of the universe and was connecting with some of the masters on a very high level. I was not able to see what she was seeing, and when trying to do so, I saw the color salmon and then a flamingo. I thought to myself how silly is this and hesitated to tell the group what I saw. When I got home that evening, I looked up this vision in the book

Animal Wise by Ted Andrews. I read the following about flamingos, which put a rest to my vivid imagination. I quote:

> "There are ten levels on the **Tree Of Life** and each level on the tree has four worlds or dimensions. One of the four worlds is Yetzirah, or the world of formation, where the energy of things begins to take shape or form. It is in this realm that the choirs of *angels* are found who work to manifest energy into reality. At the *heart* of the Tree of Life is the level known as Tiphareth, the center for healing. Tiphareth, in the world of Yetzirah, has the color **salmon pink** like that of the **flamingo** [emphasis added]. Like the flamingo, this is where the flittering energies of new healing begin to occur. We begin to see what will benefit us and our hearts and what will not. Like the flamingo, we begin to filter through the things of the heart, especially that which may not be of benefit. In this world are found the ancient Malachim, a group of *angels* known as the miracle workers who work under the guidance of the archangel Raphael, the keeper of the Holy Grail, which lives within the heart of us all. Through the **flamingo**, we open to that which is most sacred to our hearts."

Once I read this, I had a much better understanding that although I was not seeing the Masters and archangels as Jayne was, I was experiencing them in a different manner, one that was more in tune with my gifts and understanding. This experience and revelation taught Jayne and me to honor ourselves and the signs we receive—no matter how silly they may seem. It also taught us that we are like Twin Souls: we both see corresponding energy in our own way. What one doesn't see the other one does.

~

Knock, Knock, Who's There? *(Visitations)*

Not only does the Force connect with us regularly, our spiritual family and friends also seek to touch us. I am sure that you have heard of ghosts or deceased family members doing unusual things. This is their way of sending their love and telling us that they have not forgotten about us; they are just here on another dimension, watching over us. If something happens in your life, you are probably correct in concluding who it is that is trying to reach you: usually it is accurately the first thought or person that comes into your mind.

After Deanna died, I was downstairs in the dance studio working on a dance routine. I was sitting on a stool and had just finished writing down part of the dance. I set the pencil and paper I was using down on top of the stool. As I began to walk away to continue to make up dance steps, the pencil went flying up in the air and bounced off the paper and landed on the floor. Right away, I thought of Deanna playing tricks on me.

One day, I was feeling down, was upset about something, and I was crying while making my daughter's bed. (She had a stuffed dog that sat on the top of her headboard. It was wedged tightly between the headboard and the wall.) I had just gone down to the foot of the bed to tuck in the sheets and the stuffed animal came off the headboard, flew up in the air, and bounced on the bed. My first thought was my dad who was always the jokester in the family. I started to laugh, and of course I had stopped crying, dad's way of making me realize that life is too short to be crying over things of little importance.

One evening while sleeping, I opened my eyes in the middle of the night to see a small dog jumping up and down by the side of the bed. It was so real to me that I pushed Bob who was sleeping next to me and said "Who let a dog in the house?" He flipped on the light and of course when I looked again it was gone. The dog looked just like my old dog, Snoopy, who I am sure had come to visit me.

~

Weird Science
(Supernatural Phenomena, Electronics, Energy)

From the time that I was a little girl, I have always caused wristwatches to malfunction. If a watch given to me would run for more than a week before breaking, I was lucky. After going through a few watches, my parents finally stopped buying them for me. When I was old enough to buy a watch for myself, I had the same trouble. I could not understand this pattern until one day someone told me that the stopping power might derive from the electromagnetic energy that my body gave off. I found that I could use a watch harmlessly as long as it did not come into close contact with my skin. But that's not convenient for telling time, and also, that revelation apparently didn't stop me from breaking down other electronic gadgets throughout my life, including TV sets, VCRs, and a variety of other equipment.

I was preparing a workshop shortly after 9/11 in 2001. I was on the computer and had just written up the song Amazing Grace with the words in Cherokee underneath each line. I was not connected to the Internet or any other source. I hit the print button to print out the song; the printer chugged away normally. All seemed well until I looked at the print out. The computer had not printed out the words to the song at all. It had printed a picture of the American flag blowing in the breeze; it looked like water flowing and on the flag were floating lotus flowers. It was so beautiful, and I was in awe. I went to print out the words I had typed again and this time it came out fine. What a beautiful, and unexpected, message Spirit had sent.

Even my emails have given me messages from Spirit. One time I re-received a series of emails that had been sent to me in the past, with random dates and times over a 3-year period. These emails had long been deleted. The interesting part about these emails is that they were from a variety of different people, and they were all exceptionally spiritual in content—even for me. To this day, no one has been able to explain to me how a series of fourteen random spiritual emails from a 3-year period of time were returned to me all at once. I guess it is just another way that Spirit is letting me know that these people love me and are with me.

My brother and I had worked very hard to get things taken care of with my mom's house and belongings after she died. I thought it would be nice if I bought my brother a gift to thank him for his love and for working so hard with me. I wanted the gift to be very special, but since my brother and I had not been very close for so long, I really had no idea what to get him. Finally, an idea came into my mind: I thought I would buy him a silver or gold lighter. I went to a smoke shop with a friend, not having any idea what something like this would cost and was shocked to see that most lighters of this quality were selling for hundreds of dollars. I looked at one of the cheapest lighters going for $250.00. I handed it back to the man and looked at my friend and said I don't know what to do: I would love to buy this for my brother, but it costs so much money. I knew I would have a hard time trying to come up with another idea for him and really wanted to get him this lighter. The man offered it to me for about twenty dollars less and I continued to stand there and think. Spending this kind of money on one gift was not something I normally did, and I could feel my insides churning. My friend said it really isn't a bad price for something like that. After a few more minutes, the man said that he would give me the lighter for two hundred dollars but that would be the lowest he would go. Again not knowing what to do, I stood there longer, all along sensing my body getting more and more worked up. I finally reluctantly said ok and took out my charge card to pay for it. The man went to ring it up on the charge machine and found not only was the charge machine not working, neither was the cash register, or his computer. He looked at me and said he had never had this happen before and told me that if I gave him cash he would give me the lighter for $180.00. I told him that I did not have that kind of money on me, and he said that there was a bank next door where I could withdraw the money with a debit card, something I also didn't have. My friend offered to use her card, and we ran next door for the cash. We were gone no longer than five minutes and when we returned the man's machines were all working. He gave us the lighter for $180.00. Thank you Spirit!

Although I have not been able to regularly see spirits, I have been able to sense them around me. I have had proof of this by photos that have been taken with orbs or lights in the pictures that I was not able to see with my naked eye. Many people have been able to take pictures of spirit energies with their cameras, and we were no exception. Bob and I over the years have had a lot of fun going around taking pictures of areas where I personally have sensed spiritual presence; shortly after, when the film was developed, we have received truly amazing results.

~

Healings... Nothing More Than Healings
(Crystals, Healings, Reiki)

Healing work has always been of interest to me. I have taken Reiki I and II courses and have performed many healings in my life. I do believe that effectiveness is not necessarily determined by the technique one might use when healing, but rather by the intent and extent of knowing that the healing is coming from a higher source to heal the individual at the appropriate time. There are many things on this earth that have been given to us by the universe to use for healing, and I feel that we as humans haven't even begun to take advantage of the natural healing gifts that this planet has to offer. I pray that in time we will discover the myriad of natural gifts on this earth and learn how to use them to heal not only us, but also this beautiful planet of ours.

Crystals have always been of interest to me, and they are still a subject that I would love to learn more about. I have worked with a few of them over the years and found their healing qualities to be of tremendous help to me. I have found it helpful to have a good healing crystal book in my possession that explains what the crystal is, its properties, and its healing essence. Over the years, I have cleared sinus congestion, improved my creativity, reduced my fibroids, brought more clarity into my meditations, and projected healing energy into a room by using crystals.

For a long time, ever since I was 38, I have had problems with my digestion. I had no idea what caused my problems, but I began to be very careful about what I ate. Sometimes, even the smallest thing would upset my stomach, and it has caused me to miss out on really being able to enjoy food the way that I would like to, especially when I have gone to weddings or barbeques. I was often hardly able to eat, from fear of being in the bathroom for the rest of the night. One year, when I was in Virginia, Ellie connected to the Force. The following is a copy of what happened, transcribed from the actual taped session ("Chris" is me).

CHRIS: I have a question. I have had problems with digestion for a long time now. Is there any particular reason *why*, that you could tell me, that might help me?

TEACHER: There is an energy, my dear, within yourself that you feel in some way that the wholeness of yourself is not complete. Is that not correct?

CHRIS: Yes

TEACHER: And therefore it is within the physical form that is reaching out trying to create a wholeness within the physical form. Do you understand that?

CHRIS: Yes

TEACHER: But the fullness of which you desire, you have now gravitated around you. The energies of which you have now brought into your energy factor are trying to create that wholeness. And it will manifest because it is their desire as well as yours. To assure yourself, both in your physical and your etheric, of the wholeness and well-being of your physical form. It is important here to address, with you among others who have created this image, that the work that lies before you must be done with a wholeness and a feeling of well-being. Do you understand that?

CHRIS: Yes

TEACHER: It is your creativity that has been intertwined within the evolvement of which you have come to know. And therefore as you begin to release and allow this energy to penetrate, it will fill the rather small energy holes within the physical form. It is as if the inner confounds of the physical form have almost felt an undeveloped avenue. Do you understand that?

CHRIS: I think so.

TEACHER: And therefore you have been reaching out to create around you people who can penetrate within the physical body to begin to seal and heal. It is occurring, but there must be that complete release of some energy factors that still remain embedded within the depths of your inner thoughts. I do not need to reveal any further than that for I do feel you do understand of what I am addressing to you. Is that not correct?

CHRIS: I think I have a pretty good idea. Yes, I am trying very hard to work on it.

TEACHER: Try. Do not be so stressful of working on it specifically yourself. What you must do as an individual is to begin to relax in the environment in which you are. Would you like to accept a challenge?

CHRIS: Sure

TEACHER: I am speaking to the group.

GROUP: Yes

TEACHER: Would you like to see a manifestation.

GROUP: Yes

TEACHER: Shall we try?

GROUP: Yes

TEACHER: I want this individual of whom I am speaking, to walk into the center of the room.

CHRIS: I am here

TEACHER: I want you each now in your own highest truth to begin to manifest a gold rose. Begin to see the petals and see this individual standing in the middle of this rose. Good! Bring the petals out stronger, put your strength into them. And you who stand in the middle, my dear, just relax. Just relax. Are you relaxed?

CHRIS: I'm trying.

TEACHER: I know you're a little nervous, aren't you?

CHRIS: Yes

TEACHER: But, my dear, allow a manifestation to happen. Just relax. Just relax. Just relax. And as she is, the rest of you begin to put a deep gold in every petal around her. See yourselves individually as a bud who is now open widely. And blow your pollen into the center of this rose. Physically blow your pollen. Now just allow her to stand in this essence. I want you to feel the tingling within your body. I want you to seal the wholeness within your physical form. I want you to take the essence of these petals. Bring it up through your feet. And allow it to permeate within your physical form. Now all the seeds of health and growth are now within you. At the moment of stress, visualize in your mind, the seed bursting in to this flower of which you standing in. Do you feel the sensation?

CHRIS: Yes

TEACHER: Do you know that you are loved?

CHRIS: Yes

TEACHER: Do you know that you are pure of heart.

CHRIS: Yes

TEACHER: Do you know those that surround you now gaze upon
you in your full truth?

CHRIS: Yes

TEACHER: Then my dear, know that you are healed.

CHRIS: Thank you

TEACHER: Now may I ask each of you, how did that feel to you?

GROUP: Wonderful

TEACHER: Were you able to visualize this individual in the center?

GROUP: Yes

TEACHER: Were you able to see the strength that you gave the
petals?

GROUP: Yes

TEACHER: Ah, but to address the question that we were asked
before about clarity of love....

GROUP: Yes

TEACHER: Do you remember that?

GROUP: Yes

TEACHER: What did you do? You took the seed or the essence of your very being without question, without doubt and did what?

AN INDIVIDUAL IN GROUP: We extended it, we presented it.

TEACHER: Is that clarity of love?

GROUP: Yes

~

Since that day, I have been able to eat almost anything I like without getting sick, and I have finally been able to enjoy my life more fully thanks to my loving spiritual friends and the Force.

~

Life In The Fast Lane *(Time Travel)*

This is one area where I personally have not had a lot of experience, but I do know of many people who have been lost and have miraculously found their way to where they have wanted to go, or they became lost and ended up where they wanted to be in the same amount of time as if they had never been lost in the first place. I am not sure why or how this happens; I only know that there have been a few times in my life where I was going somewhere, running quite late, and found myself at my destination on time or earlier. I have no explanation of how time just seemed to change, but it did.

Jayne and I have had this happen to us a few times. Once, when we were running about 15 minutes behind trying to meet up with a friend, that 15-minute ride lasted 5 minutes. We didn't make all the green lights; we didn't drive faster than usual; we just ended up where we needed to be when we needed to be there (something that in earthly terms might be comparable to 'making it there in record time...and then some!' minus the feeling of exhaustion that comes from rushing).   Spirit can work in strange ways.

~

One Way Or Another *(Synchronicity)*

Synchronicity is a series of fortunately timed, galactically coordinated events that takes place in our lives, events in which we are guided by Spirit to or through the places and occurrences that we need to experience, places where blessings prevail with little or no effort on our part. I position this section here, last, because it is what I believe to be the most profound example of the Divine working through us and changing our lives, giving us grace, and giving us the blessings that we need, even when we don't expect them. Although I describe here two interesting events, I would like it to be known to my readers that what I have learned from this is that Spirit moves through our lives when we *ask* and when we are prepared to accept and *let go* of our fears.

I had been suffering with hot flashes, certainly something that many women have experienced. Being holistically inclined, I was determined to find a way to cure myself without using drugs (since medications usually made me sick because of my sensitive stomach). I started with all the basics, eating better foods, vitamins, minerals and any natural herb blend that I could get my hands on. Each one had the same results: my hot flashes went from one every two hours to one every 20 minutes. I then tried acupuncture, Reiki, massage, chiropractic care and Chinese medicines—again, all to have the hot flashes increase. After two years of suffering and very little sleep, I finally resigned myself to go to the doctor and go on some kind of hormone replacement therapy. I found that this was not possible for me since I had uterine fibroids. The doctor said that hormone therapy could increase the fibroids' growth.

I felt like I was "between a rock and a hard place." I signed up for a class at Walt Whitman High School to learn about stress reduction in-time for the fall adult education classes that I taught, and maybe to help me reduce stress in my life. I also skimmed a book on Bach Flower Essences, which confused me and went over my head. In the spring of 2005, while packing for a trip to see my son, Nick, in California, I was staring at my bookshelf trying to decide what book to take with me to read on the trip. I finally chose a book that I had bought the fall before on what I thought was "Dowsing" (originally an old form of using two metal rods to find underground water and more recently also related to using a pendulum to connect to the Spirit world via asking questions). The book was called M.A.P. I ended up never looking at the book the whole time I was in California.

We were packing to come home, and I had placed the book in the bottom of my suitcase, figuring that I would not look at it on the way home at this point either. At the last minute, for some unknown reason, I decided to take the book out of my suitcase and put it in my carry-on. On the plane, Bob and the lady next to him were watching an interesting show, so I went to plug my headset in so I could see it too. The plug on the headset fell out, and I tried again with no luck. I tried to see why it wasn't staying in and even tried holding it in with my finger only to find the reception fading in and out. I put the headset away, and had Bob hand me my book. I started to read and was amazed at what I read. I found in the first chapter that the M.A.P book had little to do with dowsing; it actually stood for Medical Assistance Program. As I continued to read, the writer basically said that he was not trying to convince people to only use this program; however, if you were the type of person who had been to doctors and tried this and that and had found yourself "Between A Rock and A Hard Place," this could be the program for you.

I was shocked; these were the exact words that I had used to describe how disgusted I was at not finding an answer to my problem. I read on and also found that the writer suggests using Bach Flower Essences to enhance the program. "Oh MY!" I thought. I was just trying to learn about them. Of course I was excited; I finally felt that there was some hope for what I was going through.

I told a friend about this unusual synchronicity on the way to a meditation in New York City one day, and she said that she had heard of the M.A.P. program but didn't know anything about it. She wanted to learn more. I told her that the book was hard to get—it had been out of print since 1994. We got to the city and once at the small meditation center, my friend went for a brief peak into the center's tiny bookstore. Lo and behold on the shelf was one M.A.P. book. She came running out to show me, and we both laughed at how she had manifested what she wanted so fast. What were the chances of that one M.A.P. book that was so hard for me to find being on the shelf?

Obviously, it was meant to be. I continued to read the book myself, telling Jayne about the fact that I might want to borrow back her Bach Essence Book. I found more information online on Bach Flower Essences.

[Dr. Bach had taken flowers and plants and floated them in water placing them in the sun. As the sun heated the water, the flower essence would mix in the water, after which all of the flower or plant would be removed, leaving only the essence behind. These essences, which were developed in the late 1920's to early 1930's, are a vital part of maintaining a healthy balance; they address emotional and attitudinal reactions to stress and turn negative emotions into positive ones, thus decreasing stress, increasing immune system function and aiding in the body's natural ability to heal.]

As I began to understand a little more about how they worked, I also realized that you could try and pick—to address your own particular situation—one or more of the 38 original essences, but it wasn't easy to do that on your own and I told this to Jayne. She went, without my knowing it, to the library to see if there was a Bach Flower Essence practitioner on Long Island. She found one all right:

It turned out to be the **same** lady that was teaching the **stress reduction** class that we had already signed up for.

We went to the class, and Jayne and I learned more about the essences; the lady who ran the class gave us

Rescue Remedy (five of the Bach Flower Essences blended together to make a formula). She told us to go home and use it for a week. I started taking it that night. In one day, I felt more relaxed; in two days, I was sleeping better; in three, days my hot flashes had decreased tremendously, and by the end of the week, I felt better than I had in two years. The following class, the lady made us up our own formula, and that too helped me with feeling more balanced in my life. To date, I have done the meditation work with the M.A.P. program and used the flower essences, both of which have helped me. I have been able to handle and take on some of the things that before were challenges in my life, and I have found amazing results. I thank God that he guided me to and through this holistic way of healing myself without using drugs, since I do believe natural remedies are less invasive and a more healthy way to heal the body. I feel very blessed and know that this set of experiences was pure synchronicity.

~

More on synchronicity...

Because of the chaos that has occurred in my life, I have lost many of my childhood possessions. One of those possessions was a book that my dad used to read to me when I went to bed at night. It was a poem book with beautiful pictures in it, and I can remember always falling off to sleep into a beautiful children's fantasy world when listening to these poems.

In recent days, when I no longer owned the book but would often think about it, I could not remember the book's title or the author. One day when meditating, I saw myself walking along the water in a flowing white dress. When I told Jayne of the meditation, she said that the flowing white dress reminded her of my daughter Holly and how beautiful she was. I told Holly about the meditation and what Jayne had said, hoping to make her feel better about herself (the day before, she was feeling unhappy with the way that she looked.) Holly told me that my story was funny because the image in my meditation reminded her of a favorite picture that she had loved since junior high (Holly was 29 at the time of this conversation). I said to her: can you find the picture on the Internet and show it to me?

Holly went online to try and look for the picture and brought up the artist's web site and the picture that she loved. It was a beautiful rendering of a woman standing on a mountaintop, in a flowing dress that was blowing in the breeze, with her arms wrapped around her head. It was certainly a striking picture. I asked Holly to please bring up the other pictures on this website. I was sure there were probably others I would love to see. As she did, I was amazed to see that there were a few that I recognized as pictures from my childhood poem book. Holly then proceeded to see what books the artist had illustrated and lo-and-behold; we found the name of the poem book that I had been looking for. I was able to find the book "Poems of Childhood" by Eugene Field, illustrated by Maxwell Parish, offered by a British company at a good price. The only little hurdle was going to be paying for the shipping, but that was taken care of for me too, since Holly's boyfriend Simon (from England) was kind enough to bid on the book for me, win the bid, and mail the book out to me. I can't tell you how happy I was to have my old book again. It really touched my heart. Thank you Spirit, Jayne, Holly, and Simon.

~

Blessings, abundance, enduring joy, and spontaneous happiness have been ways that the Universe has blessed me. My gifts are constantly improving, and new gifts are continually being brought into my life. As I practice, read, learn, and remain open-minded, each day becomes a joyful journey full of interesting experiences and unexpected turns.

Each new experience has not always been the one that I was expecting, but I continually try to remain open to what path Spirit prompts me to take (or make), even if it is not the path I wished for. I feel that as I live my life, I am becoming more aware of the power of Spirit, the power of my Self, and the protection of the Universal energies that guide me each day. For they (not I) are aware of what my future holds, and if I can trust in that and believe that they know what is best for my highest good, I find that I am always guided and led in the direction of my soul's deepest desires. So, I continue to pay attention to the signs, and I allow myself to be consciously aware of, and to receive the many daily blessings that come from, the Power within and above.

(Channeled by the author)

The lasting peace you feel at times
removes any doubt in your mind.
Trust your concepts, and actualizations
and allow the eons of time to
begin to manifest.
The situation and the dynamics that
present themselves to you in intimate details
show you what you are about to embark on.
This is not the only reason for your existence.
This is the innermost core of the pattern of mind
and spirit interacting with each other
in an effort to embark on a new journey
in this time and space.
Fear not that we will be by your side,
for your fortitude and determination
will envelop your thoughts or the internal shift
that you sometimes feel.
There is one important message
that We must give to you
and that is to always trust your inner being
and know that life is just the truth which is

written and derived by the people of this earth.
It may not be your inner truth, your inner being,
for life is eternally yours.
Rest when you can;
healing will come over you,
and grant you all of the strength and power
that you need to accomplish your desires.

Chapter Thirteen

We come into this world full of love and hope, pure and innocent, and unaware of what life holds for us.

Often our journeys—like the journey described in this book—begin with the love that we receive from our parents or guardians, who most of the time, are sure that they know what is best for us. They try to protect us with their love by teaching us how to live our lives. They give us rules to follow, and guide our steps, hoping that with each one we take, we will live a joyful and happy life. Most of the time, innocently enough, our parents do not realize that they can not always protect us, and that their truths and what they have learned, may have worked well for them, but may not work for us.

For many: the joy of our younger years changes; we get older; we rebel; and we begin our own journey, our own search. A search that leads us down many paths looking for hope, looking for love, and perhaps most of all, looking for our own truths. We seek answers to the questions that nag at our souls, personal ones, and deep-rooted ones, that are even hard for us to express. We are taught to pray, and we reach out to the heavens, yet often wonder why it seems like our prayers are not being answered. We sometimes ask God if He has left us on this God Forsaken Place called Earth to suffer and fend for ourselves. What our parents, with all their good intentions, didn't know or hadn't taught most of us, is that the answers to our questions lie within us, that the guidance and help we may need is not only a moment away, but lovingly being sent to us if we can stop long enough to look at our surroundings and the messages that the spirit world is sending and is waiting for us to receive internally.

Some of us give up hope; others of us touch heaven's apron strings, finding a moment's joy only to have our feelings of trust and hope dashed. We struggle and fight for peace, for freedom, and for a release from the problems that confine us. As hard as it is to accept, I do believe that through all of our personal trials, we ARE on our own proper course: The one that each of us must take—the path that we choose—before we come here. The rough roads and hard journeys that we face in life are blessings in disguise and teach us to be strong, giving us the courage that we need to face and overcome our fears and uncertainties.

Our current technological culture does not recognize death and transformation. We do not want to talk about "the end" and don't realize that ends are also beginnings. All forms change, age becomes youth, death becomes life, and disease becomes health. We need to be aware of the fact that you can only "have" as long as you "care for." We must give to—and take care of—our bodies, relationships, and gifts. This is what keeps it all going. If you leave it alone without your spiritual consciousness, it will be gone and changed into something else.

We all are searching for something; we all want to be loved; we all want to be valued and nurtured. We all hope our lives have some meaning and we pray not only to understand why we are here, but we hope to leave our mark on the world. We try and control our life journey instead of living our lives to the fullest, appreciating who we are, and living in the moment. Do we ever stop and consider what OUR hopes and dreams truly are? Do we stress ourselves out, trying to accomplish certain goals or find the answers to these questions? Life should be joyful, not stressful.

To have, you must hold.
Hold gently and kindly in your mind
the image of love for all beings and things.
They then will live for you and give you life.

Throughout this book, I have inserted spiritual questions, for I have tried not only to give my readers my experience of things, but pivotally also to ask questions that would hopefully open my readers' minds, give them new insights and outlooks, and if they choose, they too can find the answers that they search for through the unlimited resources that are there for each of us.

In the closing pages of this book, I would like to end with the positive blessings of my life journey and my personal insight into my future and into the world's.

I do believe that I wanted the control of my life; I wanted always to have my hands on the wheel, and it was hard for me to give some of this control to the universal powers that be, trusting that my life's path would always have a positive outcome. The more that I learned, the more that I let go and let God, the more peaceful my life became, and the more joyful each day turned out.

Let me be clear: I still have my stressful moments. We are always growing from the hard times that are handed to us. The thing is: I am now more aware of the stress that I put on myself and have learned how to better deal with it—even to use it toward my deepest fulfillment. As time goes on, I find that although I may get out of sorts, no ripple burdens me or lasts for long. I have learned to honor myself and my needs, realizing that doing so is not an act of selfishness, but a way of strengthening my inner being, a way of making it easier to connect to Divine Spirit and to make the most of life's moments.

I, like many, thought that the grass was greener on the other side. I realize now that I was blessed to be adopted into a family who gave love to the best of their ability. I know now that I certainly would never have been the person I am today or have accomplished what I have accomplished if I had been brought up by the mother who gave birth to me. I thank her for giving me up for adoption, giving me the chance and the resources to achieve what I have achieved and setting me on a path to live my life to the fullest. I know that my delicate spirit would probably have suffered indescribably in an atmosphere of upheaval and uncertainty. I feel blessed to have received much love and support in my life from multiple family members and friends. I know that I am surrounded by love even when I am alone. I am not afraid of what my future may hold, for I know Divine Presence is always with me. Most importantly I have learned to honor and respect the person who I am and that I have become.

To date May 23, 2006, Holly has become a cancer survivor, among many other miraculous traits of her beingness and journey. She is a beautiful, healthy, and accomplished woman. She has been married, divorced, and is enjoying her life to its fullest. She means the world to me, and I feel blessed to have her for my daughter. She has brought beauty, compassion, joy, humor, and love into my life. We have grown to respect, honor, and cherish our times together, for we both have learned that you never can know what tomorrow might bring. I know that we have been together in many lifetimes before, and there is no doubt in my mind that we have supported each other in this lifetime as well as in others before. I am honored to be Holly's mother and continue to wish her love and blessings in her life.

Nicholas, my son, has made me so proud. He has struggled through his life with many burdens, and yet has found the strength, repeatedly, to accomplish and move forward into a life of independence, adventure, compassion, generosity and love. I admire his strength, perseverance, and intelligence. He is well-liked and appreciated by each person he meets. In fact, in his independence, Nick has become a treasured being to many people in his community. I am pleased that we have grown closer with renewed respect for our individual ideas and musings on life's purpose. My son has opened my mind to new thoughts and concepts, and I have learned much from him.

Bob and I continue to grow. Our relationship of 32 years has not always been easy, but has consistently been full of love, understanding, and compassion. Bob continually touches & finds his own inner hope even as he participates meaningfully in my continued spiritual growth—a journey that has also become a part of his life and soul. We have increasingly developed similar interests, and we greatly look forward to traveling, building labyrinths, giving to the spiritual community, and experiencing new and wonderful adventures together.

Although Miss Jen is the director of the dance studio, it continues to run from my home, and I continue to teach dance to adults once or twice a week. I am still building labyrinths in my yard twice each year, and I welcome all who are interested in walking this vortex of life. The personal energy and inner power of the labyrinth is there for anyone who enters to discover. It has been revealed that in a past life, I helped develop these amazing geometric sacred shapes, and I hold this knowledge within my soul which is fulfilled each time I create a labyrinth and watch each soul who enters walk its path. I continue to write my poems, which are inspired by Spirit.

When the opportunity arises, I am happy to share my experiences with others in order to give them my love and hope for the future. For I am a humanitarian, and it is important to me to help others in whatever way Spirit sees fit for me to work.

Jayne and I continue to hold workshops and work together to enhance our own personal gifts using many modalities to embrace the blessings that have been given to us by Spirit. One of the things that I look forward to and enjoy each year with Jayne is going down to Virginia. There, we join Ellie Fristensky and other spiritually-minded people. Ellie usually does her trans-channeling, and I am honored to be a part of this experience. She usually channels in one of the Masters and also one who we have known for years who we call 'Teacher'. Teacher patiently answers the many questions we hold within. Last October, we again met and listened to the Force speak to us. Their message this year was very profound, and I will share some of their message here as I understand it. This was our ninth reunion, and the Force told us that we have all grown spiritually. They say that we have become strong pillars of light to our world and because of our growth, Teacher too has moved forward into a new vibrational level. This was wonderful to hear. For we forget that our positive growth not only affects us personally and spiritually, but also affects those souls that interact with us.

As I speak of this here, I feel that each of us is so important to the entire growth of our world. We may say that we cannot change the world, but we can. For when each of us thinks a positive thought, says a prayer, or connects with the spirit world in some way, beings on the other side see our light. This light combines with other lights of this world, and together in our unification, we begin to make a difference in the world we live in. For I believe this: as God, the guardians, angels and the higher realms see our light shining, they are able to then connect with us, and this energy then is sent out throughout our World and begins to cleanse its very being.

You may ask why then are there so many Earthly disasters? The Force explained it to us this way. Over time, a thick cloud has covered our Earth. This cloud was formed by all the negativity that has been expressed on our Earth on many levels. Some of us are trying to help heal this world of ours with our positive intents. These intents shine as beautiful light and try to break through this dark cloud. This is our way of trying to heal our Earth (a living thing). So as the Force explained, the Earth, with our help, is trying to eliminate this negativity and is releasing this negativity through the natural disasters, which we are experiencing.

I believe that there is hope for humanity and for our Earth. I believe that we can each play a part in our Earth's healing by beginning to make positive changes in our lives. We don't need to be doing this on a large scale, for if each person in this world can begin by giving, caring, and loving others and this world, thinking positive thoughts and treating our own selves in a loving and positive manner, we can all manifest a world of peace. We each have the power within us, hidden in our souls (perfection), that waits for us to feel it, sense it and touch its inner being. I do believe that we can manifest the things that we need in our lives with positive intent and love.

So I purposely make this book thirteen chapters—a number that to many has been negative, evil, or superstitious—for the things that were my truths as a child and the fears that belonged to others that were passed down to me are no longer a part of my energy. I have found the power within me to speak my own truth and to share my love and positive intention with others.

I write this book and my story in order to heal myself and those who read it. Much love and positive energy has gone into this book, and it has been written from the heart, not sensationalized in any way.

Always remember that you are a blessing to this earth, and are never alone or abandoned in any way. For you have a family, a spiritual family, whose energy is there to touch. All you have to do is open yourself up to their love, to their light, and to ask for strength and guidance.

Kathy Jane Segur, Christine Diane Higgins, Christine Guardiano: Yes, to **all** of these names I will still indeed answer. But no longer out of confusion or separation from my 'true' identity. Instead, I answer to all, peacefully grounded in the firm and beautiful first-hand knowledge of the profound Unity of all things—of the perfection of my own path. I honor all experiences that have made me who I am.

Together with love, we can all heal our fears, our health and our lives. Let us change this world together and continue to Grow In Light.

~

Epilogue
by Holly

I have always wanted the opportunity to write an epilogue to a book, but always thought they would be the words elucidating my own published work. Although life has not yet given me that particular chance, energy, or the time to accomplish that particular achievement, I feel incredibly grateful for this unprecedented—and cherished—opportunity to join written words with the work of my own mother.

I am a writer by hobby, and, like my mom growing up, I always wrote in moments of sadness and confusion, hoping for answers to life's questions that may come from using writing as my outlet. It is something I've done since I was as little as I can remember.

I was about the age of twelve when I wrote my first poem while I sat in a gymnasium, watching my mother take a dance class. I wrote the poem in less than an hour and to this day, she still has that poem. Probably because it was about her and how much she meant to me. I had such an inspiration then, sitting there. Feeling the music's beat through the hardwood floor as I wrote in my bound notebook, I saw my mother so gracefully dance and move to the rhythm. It was a school project. It wasn't supposed to be more than a few lines or about anything special, but that moment grabbed me so hard and showed me something that I had never seen before. It showed me how lucky I was to have a woman so beautiful in my life. To have someone who not only brought me into this world, but who helped me through it and would be there for me no matter what happened. To have a woman who would've given her life up for me if she had to because I was everything to her.... I knew this, and I barely knew her then. We didn't get along really then, didn't speak much at all because I was the common, angry adolescent who didn't need anyone because I had it all figured out. God, only if I knew then what I know now.

What I know now: inspiration, including inspiration from my mom, is my life. My mother is everything to me. Without her, I would be nothing. She has shown me things that no one else could have ever shown me. She has taught me things that no teacher could teach me. She has been there for me through everything, more than I have ever wanted her to be—because I was afraid, worried, or sad. I didn't want her to have to go through what I was going through or be dragged along for the ride, but I truly knew deep down that she would never trade the experience of doing this, for the world. That no matter what curve ball was thrown at me or what disaster faced me, she would want to be a part of my life because she loved me. And the love... they say that a mother/daughter's love is something that no one can ever comprehend. They say that it's so strong and powerful that nothing can break it—that you don't know what it's like until you have it. And that's what we finally have.

So, it's been about 18 years now since I sat there in awe in that gym, watching my mother's every move like she was the most beautiful angel flying through the sky from cloud to cloud. She was mesmerizing to me, almost hypnotizing. The words I jotted down came out so easily, almost as if I was translating them from an outside source. I was writing them down, but so effortlessly that I knew it was she who caused one of the most inspirational moments in my life. She was the reason that I knew I had "that special something" about myself. Her performance and ability that evening brought it out for all to see, especially to the person who mattered the most... me.

I will always treasure that moment and never forget it because I was finally able to see my mother how I had always wanted to see her. She is the woman who is my role model, my best friend, my savior, and my strength. She is the most intelligent, creative, and amazing woman I have ever set my eyes on. Her soul and spirit translates to greatness, sincerity, and kindness. She is everything I want to be now and everything I want to grow up to be. She is the world to me and she is my inspiration.

And now she has completed her story, her book, and she has asked me to add a few of my own words into it. I sit here wondering what I can possibly say, and I almost feel as though nothing I write here can even come close to what I have read in this book. I always knew that my mother's life was full of happiness and pain, but the few stories that she was willing to tell me over the years were only a minute summary of what appears in this work. I never knew all of what she has disclosed here. I never knew all of the change that she has gone through (endured and created herself). And I think, even now, after reading what's here, there is still so much left to know. But the fact remains that the pieces that my mother can share are all here—open to the world for _all_ to enjoy—and that takes a lot of strength, courage, and inner peace to accomplish. And it's these little steps in life that make everything possible... tell a little, share a little, explain a little, and eventually all falls into place in the end.

So, the end... or "The End?" This is the end of my mother's book, but at the same time it is also the beginning. It is the end of a story, but the start to another. It is the end of an old life and the beginning of a new one.... It may be experienced as a resurrection, a growth, a rebirth.

And with the change encapsulated in this book, now nothing—and everything—has changed for me and for her.

And that is something, the only thing, we need to accept in order to be able to be free and to be happy. We need to know that change, even though it is sometimes harsh and painful, is what makes us who we are. And it is the acceptance of change that determines our fate, our destiny, our experience, and our lives.

Change will relentlessly occur. And yet we will always remain true to who we are....

~ June 25, 2006

Appendix

Christine 18 months old   *Christine 7 years old*

Christine high school   *Christine 48 years old*

Gordon and Christine Higgins▲

Robert (Bob) and Christine Guardiano

Roger R. Higgins   Doris E. Higgins

Nick Guardiano

Christine and Holly 1999 ▲

Holly and Christine 2006

NEW YORK STATE DEPARTMENT OF HEALTH ADOPTION INFORMATION REGISTRY
NON - IDENTIFYING INFORMATION REPORT

Registrant's Name: Christine D. Higgins Guardiano
Registry #: 51-028920

Non-Identifying Information: Concerning the birth parents at the time of the adoptee's birth.

ITEM	Mother	Father
Age	24	Not reported
Heritage:		
Nationality	USA	Not reported
Ethnic Background	Not reported	" "
Race	White	" "
Physical Appearance:		
Height	Not reported	Not reported
Weight	" "	" "
Hair Color	" "	" "
Eye Color	" "	" "
Skin Color	" "	" "
Other Characteristics	Not reported	Not reported
Religion	Protestant	Not reported
Education	Not reported	" "
Occupation	" "	" "
Talents, Hobbies and Interests	Not reported	Not reported

Health History of Birth Mother: The pregnancy was normal and lasted 40 weeks. You weighed 7 pounds, 4 ounces at birth. No congenital malformations were noted.

Health History of Birth Father: No information was reported.

Facts and circumstances relating to the nature and cause of the adoption: Your mother was abandoned by your father prior to your birth. The adoption was handled by Wayne County Department of Social Services.

This report was completed by: Peter M. Carucci, Director

Peter M Carucci   3/1/1999

Page 267

September 30, 1999

Christine Guardiano
42 Old East Neck Road
Melville, NY 11747-2817

Dear Segur Family,

My name is Christine Guardiano and I was adopted at 15 months old.
I was born on March 17th 1951 in Rochester, NY. The name that was
given to me at birth was Kathy Segur also known as Cathy Jane.
I am looking for medical history of my family for my children and myself.
I do not want to disrupt anyone's life and respect the privacy of my
natural birth parents, if for some reason they do not want to meet me.
I would also appreciate any nationality background information on the
name Segur since I do not know that either and it is also important for
medical reasons. If you can help my children and I in anyway I would be
extremely grateful. You can email me at GrowInLite@hotmail.com or
write me at the above address.
Thank you for your patience and understanding.

Sincerely,

Christine Guardiano

Christine Guardiano

STATE OF NEW YORK
DEPARTMENT OF HEALTH

Corning Tower   The Governor Nelson A. Rockefeller Empire State Plaza   Albany, New York 12237

Antonia C. Novello, M.D., M.P.H.
Commissioner

Dennis P. Whalen
Executive Deputy Commissioner

September 23, 1999

Ms. Christine D. Guardiano
42 Old East Neck Road
Melville, New York 11747-2817

Dear Ms. Guardiano:

This is in response to your August 12, 1999, letter to the Adoption Registry and your August 11, 1999, letter to Congressman Ackerman.

The court that handled your adoption indicates that your adoption was handled by the Wayne County Department of Social Services. That agency reported to the Adoption Registry that they had no record of your adoption. In view of this, the Adoption Registry sent you available non-identifying information reported by the court of adoption and from your original birth certificate. I have reviewed the information shared with you in my March 1, 1999, report and it accurately reflects the information supplied by the court of adoption and reported on your original birth certificate.

Since you were born in Monroe County and your adoptive parents lived in Nassau County, the Adoption Registry sent requests to the Monroe and Nassau County Departments of Social Services with the hope that one of these agencies would have information about your adoption. We have learned from these agencies that they have no record of your adoption. Regrettably, there is no further information the Adoption Registry has at its disposal. As an alternative you may wish to discuss with your attorney the possibility of petitioning the court to appoint a medical guardian to obtain the information you need.

Please let me know if you have any other questions; I can be reached at (518) 474-3055.

Sincerely,

Peter M. Carucci
Director
Vital Records

cc: Congressman Ackerman

Page 269

October 2, 1997

Dear Holly

 As discussed in our telephone conversation of
Oct. 1, 1997, I have received a letter from Dr.
outlining his opinion and recommendation. He
notes that based on a new pathology evaluation, this
appears to be a true cancer (not a borderline tumor).
He strongly feels that surgical evaluation is needed
to determine if any spread of this cancer has
occurred.

 I strongly agree with this opinion. CT scan will
only show advanced metastatic spread, at which point
the disease would most likely be fatal. Only surgical
evaluation will find microscopic spread, at the time
when the disease is still curable.

 I strongly advise that you undergo surgical
exploration to evaluate the extent of disease so that
proper treatment can be offered. Any further delay
may allow spread of this disease to the point of being
incurable.

Sincerely,

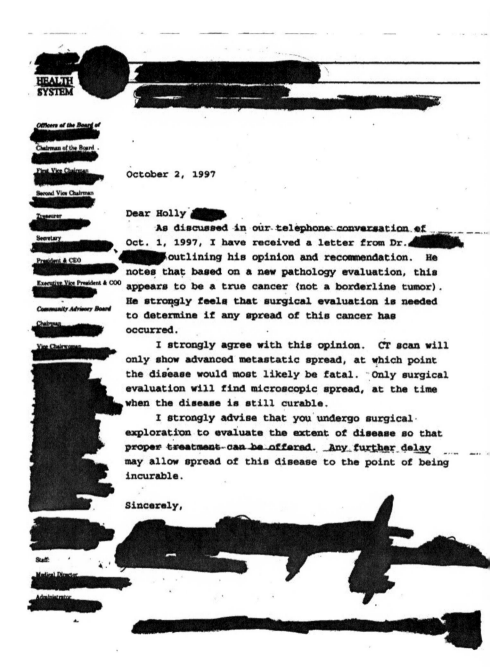

MD
Deputy Physician in Chief, Disease Management Teams
Chief, Gynecology Service, Department of Surgery
Gynecologic Oncology Research

October 27, 1997

M.D.

Re: Holly

Dear Dr.

Ms. Holly was seen in my office for a consultation and her full consultation note is enclosed. She was also presented to our Treatment Planning Conference on October 23, 1997. This conference is attended by gynecologic oncologists, medical oncologists and radiotherapists from the Gynecology Disease Management Team. This case was discussed at length with the options being exploratory laparotomy for complete surgical staging versus close follow up with physical examination and imaging studies. It was the consensus of our group that she should be followed closely and not undergo surgical restaging at this time, however, it was pointed out that surgical restaging is not an unreasonable option. Certainly, we would recommend a baseline CT scan at this time and this should be repeated in six months and if that is negative we would repeat it again in one year. Some members of our group raised the possibility of utilizing a PET scan, however, there is obviously very little data about PET scans in any type of ovarian cancer particularly a low malignant potential cancer.

Since the tumor was emptied by Trocar there is always the possibility of spillage of mucinous low malignant potential cells into the abdomen and the patient may be at risk for developing pseudomyxoma peritonei. The degree of this risk, however, is not clearly documented in the medical literature.

Thank you very much for allowing me to consult on this patient.

Sincerely,

M.D.

cc: Holly

Grave Yard Orbs and Horses

Whaley House Orbs

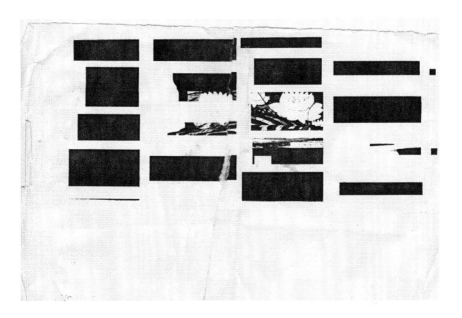

Flag / Lotus Flowers that emerged from my printer spontaneously ▲

Grave Yard Energy

How *Others* See the Author (and this book)

I have known Chris for over 20 years, and never in my life have I met anyone who looked forward to tomorrow as she does.
—Diane Luetzen

Christine's story, as it is told in this book, engrosses the reader as Christine reveals the depth of herself, making the experience not only gratifying, but an honor that she has shared so much of her true self.
—Karn McKane

Chris is my teacher, my guide and my friend. I can truly say that her spirit is a miracle and that her presence here with us is our blessing from Spirit. I have been provided a space to dance, to learn, and to grow with Chris. And I can honestly say that the course of my life has been blessed by her being here. She is an inspiration. Chris has a genuine heart and a deep understanding of things spiritual. For someone like me who thought I was alone in dealing with my abilities, I have found a place to belong. Thank you Chris
—Anna Marie May

[Christine] is fluid in movement and thought. Her journey is true, and uplifting. This book will truly be thought provoking and reassuring!
—Cindy Salemi

Chris, you bring such joy and expression to others through your talents. I will never forget the raw emotion that every labyrinth that you've created brings forth each time we go through one, no matter how different each of your creations is. You give your warmth and caring heart to every person you meet. I am one of the lucky ones.
—Cheryl Woiczechowski

How *Others* See the Author (continued)

The dictionary says, "friend(n): A person whom one knows, likes, and trusts". *My friend Chris is so much more to me. I've known Chris all of my life, I love her, and would trust her with my children's lives. She has been my rock, my inspiration, my sister. The best belly laughs of my life have been shared with her.*

How do I define friend? *I only have to use one word.............Chris.*
—Jeanine Sabatino

Chris has always been a source of joy and encouragement to me. Her positive spirit and optimism, in good times and in rough patches, have been inspirational. I've seen her confidence and self-reliance grow with each new revelation she has uncovered about herself, and I'm proud that she's part of my life.
—Laura Higgins

I have always felt that Christine was my special friend from Day One when we first met. I will never forget how supportive and kind she was to me when I was going through my divorce.
—Marilyn Aikman

Christine invites us into her journey through the dance of life, sharing her Light of Spirit with us through her creativity and experiences, reminding us that we are never alone to take that step forward on our own unique path.
—Jayne Rhodes

A troublesome and insecure childhood, together with mysterious family illnesses in her later married life, have spurred Christine on a path filled with legal roadblocks, in her attempt to locate her biological mother. As she matures, Christine blossoms in spiritual awareness, and enters a whole new world of service and exploration. A truly inspirational story.
—Cameron and Carol Higgins

How *Others* See the Author (continued)

It was inspiring that you suggest in your story that even with all of this growth, you still face challenges and stress. What has changed is your _perspective_. The way you put it is very powerful.
—Heather Cohn

Christine is a person with great insight and creative talent, but most importantly she is always willing and eager to share her gifts. This is perhaps her greatest asset as a friend and co-worker.
—Linda Zaccaro

Chris' insight and vision have created a wonderland of beauty on many occasions which has brought a tear to many eyes. Her creations have held a healing power to many people who have experienced them.
—Dottie Krug